Masters of cinema

Steven Spielberg

CAHIERS DU
CINEMA

Clélia Cohen

2

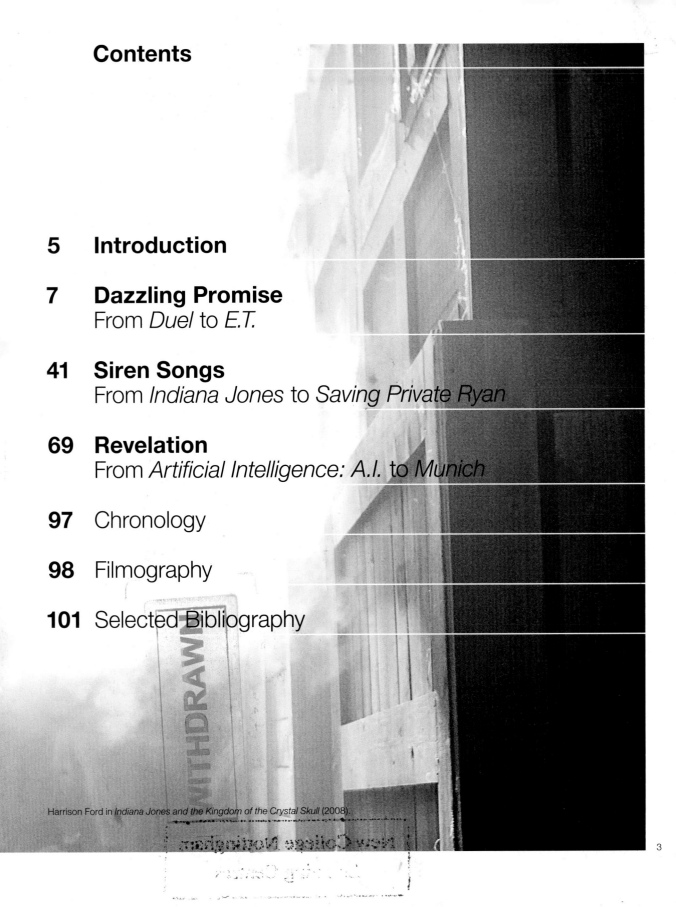

Contents

Harrison Ford in *Indiana Jones and the Kingdom of the Crystal Skull* (2008).

Introduction

The scene is a Los Angeles street, not very long ago. Steven Spielberg is walking along the sidewalk, his baseball cap jammed on his head and wearing glasses, jeans and trainers – in other words, the man who is probably the world's best-known film-maker is dressed in his usual fashion. And then a man recognizes him, comes up and addresses him: 'You know, we like your earlier films better, they were much funnier. Why can't you get back to making *E.T.* or *Raiders of the Lost Ark*?'

Spielberg himself says, 'I cannot tell you how many people come over to me on the street and repeat almost verbatim the line the Martians say to Woody Allen in *Stardust Memories*: "We like your earlier, funnier films, etc." This is not from young people but from older people, who I guess grew up with the movies I made when I was a kid and they were kids too. So I'm bewitched by Woody Allen in the sense that I keep hearing this scene from *Stardust Memories* played out in my real life. It's very bedeviling.'[1]

Spielberg trapped in a Woody Allen film? It is hard to imagine. But the films made by the director of *Close Encounters of the Third Kind* and *Jaws* have certainly changed. Since the early 2000s, the man who raised entertainment movies to their highest level (in terms of their effectiveness, thrill value and profitability) and made magic his trademark has chosen to show a darker side. His world has become increasingly disenchanted. Of all his contemporaries, including Martin Scorsese, Francis Ford Coppola and Brian De Palma, Spielberg seems finally (and against all expectations) to have established himself as the one who has come up with the most surprising, stimulating and radical offerings at the start of the twenty-first century.

So, it is a good time to revisit the career of this man of the cinema, whom French critics often categorize as a pure entertainer, and to go back in search of a connecting thread that links the child prodigy to the anxious adult, taking a very good filmmaker and turning him into a great one.

Steven Spielberg on the set of *Jurassic Park* (1993).

Dazzling Promise

From *Duel* to *E.T.*

'Hardly a single one of my films isn't based on something that happened in my childhood.'
Steven Spielberg

Cary Guffey in *Close Encounters of the Third Kind* (1977).

Steven Spielberg's childhood and youth are full of the stuff of legend. He is said to have learned to count from the number tattooed on the forearm of a relative who was a survivor of the concentration camps. And people say that for several months he would make his way into the Universal studio lot, carrying an empty briefcase, take over an unoccupied office, put his name-plate on the door and spend the day watching the films that were being shot. He is also said to have falsified his date of birth, knocking a year off so that he could achieve his long-cherished wish: to make his first film before he was twenty-one. It hardly matters whether or not that is true, but it does testify to a quite fascinating aptitude for embellishing or distorting reality in order to make it extraordinary. In short, he has a real talent for storytelling, the one area in which he has had no rivals in a career that has spanned forty years.What *is* true, on the other hand, is that before he made his first professional film, at the age of twenty-two (an episode in the *Night Gallery* series for NBC in 1969), Spielberg had already made at least twenty amateur films of various lengths, from a few minutes to two and a quarter hours, and in every genre: war movies, Westerns, cop stories and slapstick comedies. The first one, entitled *The Last Train*

Wreck, lasted three minutes. The apprentice director filmed a collision between two engines on the rails of an electric train-set his parents had given him. He 'shot and edited', as they say, stopping the camera each time he wanted to change the angle of his shot. He was eleven years old at the time.

The child prodigy

Steven Spielberg's actual date of birth, as we now know, was 18 December 1946, the place, the Jewish Hospital in Cincinnati, Ohio. As a small child he lived in a predominantly Jewish section of Cincinnati, but his parents, Leah and Arnold Spielberg, soon followed many other second-generation Jewish Americans, who gradually chose to leave the traditional ethnic neighbourhoods and apartment buildings of the old industrial cities and take the road to assimilation in the open spaces of the leafy suburbs, which with their mainly WASP populations were rapidly expanding. Spielberg's father was a software engineer, and his succession of jobs took the family westwards, each time a little nearer to Hollywood: first to Arizona, then to California in the early 1960s. Frequent moves, the almost permanent absence of a father who was always working, and the constant arguments that ended in the Spielbergs'

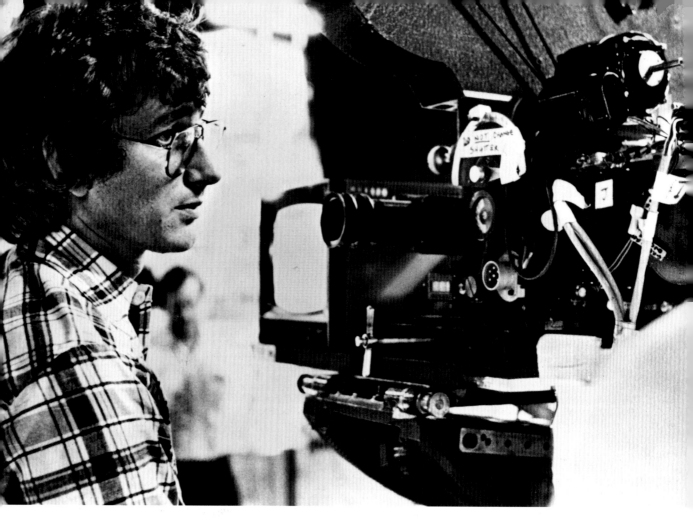

Steven Spielberg on the set of *Close Encounters of the Third Kind* (1977).

divorce in 1966, may have contributed to Steven's development into a somewhat strange child, both very talkative and rather solitary, uninterested in school, but bursting with ideas. He loved to borrow his father's little 8mm camera, using it more and more frequently until he ended up monopolizing it. In short, he was a nerd, frequently the butt of his classmates' jokes, when he was not being insulted simply because he was Jewish.

Spielberg later said that as a child he felt 'like an alien'. Joseph McBride, his main biographer, has speculated that 'his prodigious popularity [which he would achieve later] was a sign of how thoroughly assimilated he had become'.[2] He was an excluded child, but would become a universal filmmaker, erasing (at first) all traces of his Jewishness. This hypothesis may seem to place too much weight on individual psychology, but it remains true that

when he was a child, Spielberg often used his amateur films as a social weapon: by filming the kids who avoided or terrorized him, he hoped to impress or disarm them.

Television — his 'third parent', as he has described it himself — was the main cultural influence in Spielberg's childhood. He devoured Chuck Jones's cartoons, the shows of Dean Martin and Jerry Lewis, and discovered the series *The Twilight Zone*, which set the seal on his obsession with science fiction. And he read comic books— probably to the exclusion of everything else. He was a child of 1950s the pop culture, hypnotized by the television screen even when there was no picture, intrigued by what was hidden 'inside' the cathode tube. *Poltergeist* (1982), directed by Tobe Hooper and written and produced by Spielberg, in which a little girl is sucked into a television

8

Steven Spielberg (centre) in 1961.

set by mysterious forces, would later be born out of this fascination.

In terms of cinema, the films of Ford and Hitchcock made a lasting impression on Spielberg, as did the epic sweep of David Lean.[3] But at matinées in the Kiva Theatre in Scottsdale he also absorbed a vast number of B movies — westerns, Tarzan adventures and 'monster' movies — which he would immediately imitate shot for shot in the short films to which he fanatically devoted every free moment. The titles of his mini-films were already convincing, and very 'commercial'. With *Fighter Squad* (1960), he learned the tricks of editing, incorporating archive images from a documentary on World War II into material that he managed to shoot in the cockpit of a P-51 on the ground. For *Escape to Nowhere* (1962) he choreographed and filmed battles in the nearby desert, using tomato ketchup for blood. The most ambitious of these early projects was *Firelight* (1964), another 8mm science-fiction film, lasting two and a quarter hours, which contains the germ of all the themes of *Close Encounters of the Third Kind* (1977): UFOs, alienation and the desire to escape the suburbs, kidnapped children and dysfunctional families. *Firelight* was actually shown at a Phoenix cinema as part of a special evening event, when Spielberg was seventeen. The day after that showing, the Spielbergs moved to Saratoga, a small California dormitory town popular with people working in Silicon Valley. There the teenage boy had only to open his window; in front of him stretched the unfenced lawns, the ribbon-like streets, the detached homes, in short, the gently stifling conformity of American suburbia. He had found the setting for *Close Encounters of the Third Kind*, *E.T.* (1982), *Poltergeist*, or the opening scenes of *Duel* (1971).

Universal, his university

Unlike his contemporaries George Lucas, Francis Ford Coppola, Martin Scorsese and Brian De Palma, Spielberg did not attend a prestigious film school — NYU, USC or UCLA, for example. At best, he attended in a desultory manner the courses at California State University, Long Beach, where he was enrolled as a student. 'Universal Studios, in effect, was Spielberg's film school', wrote Joseph McBride. After working there as an intern in 1964 and 1965, he found a way of spending increasing amounts of time at the studio. His approach was simple: he would make contacts (he had the self-confidence of many shy people) and observe directors at work. Hitchcock was still making films there, and dozens of TV series were being shot every day. The legend of his taking over an empty office may not be literally true (although it is what McBride says, at least), but after a very short time nobody was surprised to see the person they were beginning to call 'the Kid' hanging around. Leonardo DiCaprio would do the same thing, thirty-five years later, in *Catch Me If You Can* (2002): put on a suit in order to melt into the background of his childhood fantasy.

Spielberg spent a lot of time with the editors working in the studio, and studied closely every technical step in the making of a film. He was dogged and persistent, and would show his own little creations to anyone who would look at them. But top executives were unwilling to waste their time watching 8mm films. In 1968, using funds provided by an aspiring producer, Spielberg used 35mm film to shoot *Amblin'*, a road movie about two youngsters who hitchhike to California and then go their separate ways. Its purpose was purely self-

9

promotional, and it was almost cynical in the way it picked up fashionable themes – disillusioned youth and the hippy movement – but its visual power and control were impressive. Spielberg did not have to wait long for a result: *Amblin'* caught the eye of Sid Sheinberg, the vice-president of Universal TV, who offered him a seven-year contract at $275 a week; Sheinberg would be his mentor throughout the early stages of his career.

Thus, this child of television, who dreamed of nothing but cinema, was forced to start his career on the small screen; his first commissioned work was an episode of the NBC series *Night Gallery*, entitled 'Eyes'. In making it he had to direct an intimidating *grande dame* from the old days – Joan Crawford – and the technical crew thought it was a joke when Steven Spielberg, then aged twenty-two but looking about seventeen, made his appearance on the set for the first day's filming. But his inventiveness, his bold framing and the way he rejected the fuddy-duddy conventions of television at that time (alternating medium shots and close-ups), and his fondness for continuous shots soon won them over. The episode attracted a good audience, although the studio bosses advised him to tone down his 'avant-garde' ideas a little. Between 1969 and 1973, Spielberg made a dozen films for television, playing by the rules of an old-style studio whose rigid management methods based on 'Taylorist' efficiency and time-and-motion studies were still very much those of golden-age Hollywood, and learning how to film quickly and efficiently on shoots lasting from five to sixteen days. He worked on many shows, notably the first episode of *Columbo*[4] and two episodes of *The Psychiatrist*. The second one, entitled 'Par for the Course', an intimate and astonishingly mature portrait of a man facing his imminent death, had the studio executives in tears. The reputation of Universal's precocious Kid was made. He was offered the chance to make *Duel*, which was broadcast on ABC in 1971 and given its cinema release in the following year. He made two more films for television before cinema finally called him away. Spielberg was twenty-five years old, and had missed by four years the goal he had set himself.

Steven Spielberg with Joan Crawford on the set of 'Eyes' (1969).

Pamela McMyler and Richard Levin in *Amblin'* (1968).

Opposite page: Steven Spielberg on the set of *E.T.* (1982).

Above, opposite and following pages: Dennis Weaver in *Duel* (1971).

On the road

Duel was released first in Europe, in a version that was about fifteen minutes longer than the one broadcast on television. It caused a sensation. Described by François Truffaut as a 'model first film',[5] it was the perfect stylistic exercise for the young filmmaker: on a highway in the California desert, a car with a solitary driver is pursued by a tanker with a faceless driver. With its use of the vast spaces of the American landscape, its very restricted cast of characters, and a plot that can be reduced to three lines, it is cinema at its purest. In the meticulous and relentless way he builds up the tension and suspense, Spielberg is clearly following in the steps of Hitchcock. For the role of the persecuted driver he selected Dennis Weaver, who had played the motel night clerk in Orson Welles's *Touch of Evil* (1958). And there you have Spielberg's first invocation of his great predecessors.

But he was determined to impose a style of his own, and does so right from the film's daring opening shots. In total darkness, we hear the sound of steps, a door slamming, an engine starting up.

The screen lightens, revealing the inside of a garage as a car backs out into the street. The film's long first minutes follow the route taken by this vehicle, with the camera occupying the driver's seat, from the quiet streets of a comfortable suburb to the edge of the city, and a California highway. All this is done in a series of cross-dissolves, with the car radio playing in the background. This majestic opening sequence represents not only a geographical slide from the city to the desert, but also a leap back to an earlier age in American history, the time of pursuits on horseback and 'duels in the sun'. It is almost like a flashback. Except that here the confrontation is not between man and man, but between a man-and-his-car and a headless lorry: we never see his pursuer's face. The tanker in *Duel*, dehumanized in this way, is filmed as if it were an old, vicious animal, roaring and rusty, the first of the monsters (sharks, T-Rex and Tripods) that will populate Spielberg's later films. The death of the tanker, which ends the film, is accompanied by an unusual sound effect, a strange cry emitted by the

tanker as it falls heavily into the dust: the death-rattle of a dinosaur.[6] There is a touch of cheekiness in it, the cheek of an ambitious young director, at the wheel of his flamboyant Plymouth (the car in the film), in a hurry to distance himself from the figures and methods of a cinema of dinosaurs that is coming to the end of its time. Every shot of this film, which was made in a mere sixteen days, reveals an instinctive grasp of cinematic language. Its visual purity (the red car, the blue sky, the ochre tones of the landscape), combined with a constant sensation of speed and forward movement, contributes to the dazzling limpidity of the direction. But this linear perfection is underpinned by savage and grotesque impulses that raise *Duel* above the level of a brilliant stylistic exercise. Paradoxically, we should look for the key in the identity of the hero, this ordinary man (his name is Mann) arbitrarily caught up in the chase, rather than that of his pursuer (which remains unresolved to the end). We learn, when he phones his wife from a service station at the beginning of the film, that he left home

that morning after an argument. From then on we realize that the voice of the man heard on the radio moments earlier, complaining about his bitch of a wife, was probably his own interior monologue. The long sequence in a roadside diner, in which Mann desperately scans the face of every cowboy leaning against the bar, imagining that he might perhaps be the man who is harassing him, comes close to the delirium of paranoia. And the children in the school bus, pulling faces through the rear window, look to him like unruly little gnomes. The whole story of *Duel* could therefore be read as the mental construct of a neurotic, a frustrated victim of the American way of life (house, wife and children), a product of his latent insanity. The landscape, which becomes increasingly bleak and bare, stripped of all its beauty, suggests a journey into emptiness that introduces an unexpected link with the existential westerns of Monte Hellman, *Ride in the Whirlwind* (1965) and *The Shooting* (1966).

Spielberg's first true feature film, *The Sugarland Express* (1974), is also set on the highway. But the two

road movies are very different: *Duel* has about it more of the deadly pursuit and is related, albeit distantly, to the western, whereas *The Sugarland Express* is more of a caper, closer in spirit to those American films of the 1970s that actually started in 1967 with Arthur Penn's *Bonnie and Clyde*. Lou Jean (Goldie Hawn), a delightful, maddening waif, gets her husband Clovis (William Atherton) to abscond from prison so that they can reclaim their baby, who has been placed with a foster family by social workers. In a series of situations in which each outdoes the other in incompetence, they hold up a police car, taking hostage the young cop who is driving it. The film, which was based on a true story, then speeds up like an express train, as the string of police cars following and escorting them lengthens, and in the cities they drive through, the crowds end up greeting them like rock stars, offering them gifts and provisions.

Although the overall atmosphere of the film is rather light, making its ending all the more brutal, it should not be thought that Spielberg is blind to the America he is travelling though, in this case, Texas. The background of *The Sugarland Express* is full of lynch mobs, rednecks and sclerotic bureaucracy, and it demonstrates his already marked interest in those who are marginalized, not so much socially

Opposite page: Michael Sacks in *The Sugarland Express* (1974).

Below: Spielberg during the shooting of *The Sugarland Express* (1974).

William Atherton, Goldie Hawn and Michael Sacks in *The Sugarland Express* (1974).

as geographically; Spielberg will only occasionally be an 'urban' director, and he is more interested in the intermediate zones that stretch into the distance on the outskirts of cities, than by the cities themselves. He likes to linger over a huge illuminated plastic chicken, revolving above a fast food outlet, or to have his main characters spend a night in the open in the vast parking lot of a car dealership. That particular episode provides the opportunity for two of the film's finest scenes. The first is when Lou Jean's father, who has been contacted by the police, sends his daughter a threatening message over the radio, which she does not hear since she is not in the car at that moment: 'If that man gave me a gun, I'd go down there and shoot you.' The second shows the couple, who have found a place to sleep in a caravan among the vehicles for sale, watching through its window a cartoon film (Chuck Jones's *Beep, Beep*), which is being shown on the big screen of a nearby drive-in cinema. The young man does the soundtrack for Lou Jean, but stops dead when Wile

E. Coyote falls off a cliff and is smashed to pieces, as if it is a sinister taste of things to come. There is a terrible irony here: it is a relic of childhood, a cartoon, that reminds them of death.

In neither case, does the sound (either the father's voice or the film's soundtrack) reach them. Hence this 'uninhabited' America, with its caravans, drive-ins and gas stations, is their only refuge. The teddy bear squashed flat under the wheels of passing cars in the film's final minutes is simply a confirmation: *The Sugarland Express* is a film about turbulent childhood, a theme that would go on to haunt many of Spielberg's films.

A summer in Hell
When he had almost finished shooting *The Sugarland Express*, Spielberg began to have second thoughts: his hankering after public success made him consider a happy ending. His producers, Richard Zanuck and David Brown, stood in his way, not wishing to turn what they saw as an 'auteur' film into a purely

Robert Shaw, Roy Scheider and Richard Dreyfuss in *Jaws* (1975).   Following pages: the mechanical shark, nicknamed 'Bruce', in *Jaws* (1975).

commercial product — a paradox for Hollywood! For all that, the film was a failure, but when the same producers offered him a genuinely commercial project, *Jaws* (1975), Spielberg hesitated: he did not wish to be categorized as a 'director of films about trucks and sharks', which indicates his considerable ambivalence about success.

In May 1974, Spielberg started making the film that was to change the history of American cinema. It was shot on Martha's Vineyard (standing in for Amity, the film's fictitious island), off the coast of Massachusetts, and all the conditions for a disaster were there. The weather was unpredictable, filming at sea proved dangerous, and, worst of all, the mechanical shark did not work. Bruce (that was its nickname) could not cope with water, let alone salt water, which corroded its moving parts. Interminable delays followed and on some days Spielberg shot no more than a few seconds of usable film. *Jaws* was soon dubbed 'Flaws' by the crew, its schedule shot to pieces and its initially modest

budget multiplied by three. His hands forced by circumstances, Spielberg decided to increase the effects produced by sole suggestion, which in the end is clearly what gives the film its power and ensured its success. *Jaws* is a model of precision and effectiveness, playing perversely on universal phobias: the fear of what may be hidden underwater, of course, but also the dangers to which one is exposed if one's sexuality is acknowledged too freely. The first victim, an attractive woman skinny-dipping by moonlight, bears the full impact of a voracious American puritanism, a theme that has since become a hidden subtext of horror films.

When the film was released in June 1975, it had a massive impact. Since the late 1960s, the studios had been going with the flow of the counterculture. Young directors like Dennis Hopper, Martin Scorsese, William Friedkin, Hal Ashby and Brian De Palma had gained positions of power. Strongly influenced by the French *Nouvelle Vague* (New Wave) and other European movements, they were making

Three perspectives

Some of Steven Spielberg's reflections from the 1970s. After making Jaws, *how did the thirty-year-old director see his future?*

Influences

I really like my contemporaries and can get more out of George Lucas, who's a good friend of mine, than I can by sitting in a screening room and screening eight Preston Sturges films. I mean, I really can; because at least these people are alive and living and there's a rapid exchange back and forth of scripts and ideas. I watch hundreds of old movies so don't get me wrong, but I haven't learned that much from watching old pictures. I've learned economy from John Ford. But I haven't learned economy – I'm really self-indulgent in so many ways.

But John Ford, if he's taught me anything at all, he's taught me how to hold back for an overhead shot, you know, when to go wide, when to go close – don't shoot close-ups every scene or every shot, they don't mean anything. When a close-up is good. I mean, Ford was so judicious about his close-ups and his wide-shots. Ford, technically, was, for me, the perfect filmmaker and Orson Welles was second. I only put Ford in front of Welles as a technician, as a great technician, although I've been yelled and laughed at for that.

David Helpern, *Take One*, March–April 1974, p. 13.

Jaws and style

[With *Jaws*,] I chose to make a movie that would reach audiences really on two levels. The first level was a blow to the solar plexus, and the second was an uppercut, just under the nose; it was really a one-two you're out combination, I never intended anything deeper than that, because when I read the book I had a lot of fun, and when I began reworking the screenplay I had even more fun. And I really said, I'm going to make a primal scream movie.

Richard Combs, *Sight and Sound*, Spring 1977, p. 35.

The future

I'm still trying to make a career for myself. I'm still fighting so I can be good in my eyes. When I'm good in my eyes I might even quit. I don't see that happening for years. I haven't satisfied myself with a film yet. I haven't made a film that I think is great. *Jaws, The Sugarland Express,* and *Close Encounters of the Third Kind* are not the films I could have made five years from now and hopefully as you get deeper in life and deeper in values … as I find myself caring more for people, the people around me, the people whom I love, my family, I find my films get much more personal, much more emotional, and I think that I'll be a good filmmaker when I eventually can make that turn and deal with that material and start with a personal problem and let the personal problem create the excitement.

Mitch Tuchman, *Film Comment*, January–February 1978, p. 54.

The three interviews have been collected, with a number of others, in *Steven Spielberg Interviews*, edited by Lester D. Friedman and Brent Nothbom, Jackson, University Press of Mississippi, 2000.

Jaws (1975).

Opposite page: Steven Spielberg in 1975.

films with smaller crews and with subject matter that was freer, even oppositional; this was the 'New Hollywood'. The extraordinary success of *Jaws* changed the nature of the game and began the phenomenon of blockbuster 'summer' movies, aimed at teenage audiences, which sounded the death knell of the adult, political films of the New Hollywood. At the same time, the success of *Jaws* sprang precisely from Spielberg's use of the methods advocated by the New Hollywood: location shooting, use of a hand-held camera, reinvention of the genre film, as in *The Godfather* (Coppola, 1972) and *The Exorcist* (Friedkin, 1973). What strikes one when watching *Jaws* today is the extent to which this film, the first of the blockbusters, is not at all a super-production, but more like a remarkably well-crafted B movie.

Spielberg allowed himself the luxury of filming Martha's Vineyard, a well-known holiday retreat for the Kennedys, as if it was some summer hell. For him, Hell was also to be found on the beach. Set in a charming seaside town of white clapboard houses that look as if they come out of a painting by Edward Hopper, *Jaws* is above all a great film about a fear of holidaymakers and crowds: packed beaches, suntan, fat people in bathing costumes, children shrieking … Because they are all so busy playing their annual summer games, they fail to notice that in the meantime, out at sea, Spielberg is killing a child, breaking Hollywood's last taboo. The death of the little boy on the yellow inflatable mattress will recur, like an indelible guilty memory, in Spielberg's later films, in the guise of the little drowned robot in *A.I.* (2001) or as Tom Cruise's son, kidnapped from the edge of a swimming-pool, in *Minority Report* (2002).

Roy Scheider's failure to rescue the child is underlined by an effect borrowed from Hitchcock's *Vertigo* (1958), the celebrated forward tracking shot combined with a backward zoom that leaves him standing on the sand as if paralysed, reeling from his inability to do anything. Immediately afterwards, we find him at home, sitting across the table from his youngest son, annoyed at the way he is silently imitating every gesture made by his father, who is overwhelmed, defeated and fallible. The mixture of strangeness and naturalness in this short sequence shows Spielberg's great talent for depicting scenes of family life. But he decides not to end the film on such a scene, choosing instead to show the exhausted figures of Roy Scheider and Richard Dreyfuss swimming ashore after killing the shark, rather than an emotional family reunion. Despite thumbing his nose at the box office in these ways (the death of a child, a downbeat ending), the triumph of *Jaws* ensured that the twenty-eight-year-old director was now king of Hollywood, and he was guaranteed artistic independence for a long time to come. What was he to do now, when he had the sharks of Hollywood eating out of his hand? As an obsessive worthy of the name, Spielberg lost no time in turning his hand to the longed-for remake of *Firelight*, the film about UFOs he had made when he was seventeen.

'When you wish upon a star'[7]

Close Encounters of the Third Kind (1977) and *E.T.: The Extra-Terrestrial* (1982) work as a diptych, a successive rereading of similar themes with a flavour of myth: an idealized, even messianic, vision of contact with benevolent extraterrestrial beings. We are still far from the extreme disillusionment of *War of the Worlds* (2005). While the 'encounter' itself is not quite at the core of *Close Encounters*, which is orientated more towards our anticipation of its approach,[8] it occupies the full duration of *E.T.*, which begins with the arrival of the little extraterrestrial and ends with his departure.

Both films are predominantly nocturnal, full of the starry skies of children's dreams; they mark a turn towards a cinema of magic and wonder, of haloes of light and images of cosiness and security, which would become Spielberg's signature. In *Close Encounters of the Third Kind*, we catch sight of a press cutting that reads, 'UFOs, SEEING IS BELIEVING'. *E.T.* would be a manifesto for this belief, which applies especially to cinema, of course: I believe

Melinda Dillon and Cary Guffey in *Close Encounters of the Third Kind* (1977).

what I film, I film what I believe. At this stage in his work, Spielberg is demonstrating an unshakeable faith in the image, and his shots very often have the appearance of religious images.

Close Encounters of the Third Kind starts with a burn, when the hero (played by Richard Dreyfuss, whom Spielberg hired again immediately after *Jaws*, and whom he often said at the time he saw as his alter ego) has strayed onto a dark, deserted road and sees the spaceship as it passes above his car. The beam of light that falls on his face leaves a painful mark like sunburn, a sign shared by everyone who, like him, has *seen*. Similarly, the huge cupboard in which E.T. hides is lit by a window shaped like a rose window in a church, which also sheds an unreal light. The religious symbolism is constantly there, but it is first and foremost his own ability to illuminate the world through his films that Spielberg seems to be testing. The shot that shows the small figure of a child seen from behind, standing in a doorway filled with blinding light, an imaginary place outside this world, is one that recurs emblematically in both films. At the end of *Close Encounters of the Third Kind*, when the door of the mother-ship opens to reveal multitudes of shadowy forms, their outlines are almost obliterated by the light source. The diptych thus also presents a director experimenting

with his visions, and gradually domesticating them; in *Close Encounters* they are still raw, almost too dazzling to watch, while *E.T.* presents a quieter, more subdued version, metamorphosed into a simple radiance. E.T.'s comforting presence 'warms' the child's bedroom (and his life).

But we do need to be careful; Spielberg's 'visionary' aesthetic is not necessarily naive. In both cases, contact with the extraterrestrials offers an escape route from the surrounding environment, while the ultimate 'otherness' that they represent is a good excuse to look inside our own houses. In *Close Encounters of the Third Kind*, there are two: one occupied by a single mother and her son, and the other by Richard Dreyfuss and his family. The first one is full of activity and life, without being very reassuring: toys start operating by themselves, the vacuum cleaner and cooker turn themselves on, knives fly about. The second house is run-down: Dreyfuss makes piles of earth to recreate the image of the mountain that haunts him. In *E.T.*, the house, which at first is the children's special place, is invaded near the end of the film, not by extraterrestrials but by human beings in spacesuits — scientists and FBI agents — in a terrifying descent that finally convinces us that the whole story is primarily driven by a terror of domestic life.

Some recollections by François Truffaut

I knew this film [*Close Encounters of the Third Kind*] would contain fifty minutes of special effects but I had not fully grasped the visual effect that Steven was looking for, until Douglas Trumbull (in charge of special effects) suggested I visit his workshop. That's where I understood that the film would be largely made up of superimposed images: what was happening on the ground, what was happening above people's heads and what was happening in the sky, and that all of that would take its final shape in the lab, after filming was finished, as with Alfred Hitchcock's *The Birds*. For example, I watched Douglas Trumbull filming in the following way clouds moving across the sky: he emptied packets of white

paint into an aquarium filled with warm water and filmed the way it moved at different speeds. In the film, pasted above the houses, it creates those splendid images of restless, billowing clouds that I'm sure you remember.

That visit to the special effects department made me feel humble. I understood that the role of the actor in a film of that kind was to create a stylized image, and that one had to put aside Stanislavsky's theories and become simply a shape in the tapestry.

I had admired Steven Spielberg throughout filming but when I saw the completed film, my respect for his talent increased. I understood that things that had struck me as naive on the set were, in fact, aspects of his skill. An example:

the scientists who applaud and congratulate themselves after the contact of the second kind. 'Well,' I thought during filming, 'not a very scientific attitude, and not very interesting, dramatically.' I was mistaken, because when you see the film, that moment when the scientists are applauding and congratulating themselves creates the impression of a final scene; the audience feels frustrated, they want more drama, and in fact, right after that, someone looks up at the clouds, which are becoming strangely restless and turbulent, and the film starts off again towards the famous third encounter.

I think the success of *Close Encounters of the Third Kind* comes from this very special gift for making the extraordinary

plausible. If you study the film, you'll see that Spielberg had been careful to shoot all the scenes of everyday life in a way that gives them a slight touch of the imaginary, while on the other hand, giving the 'imaginary' scenes as normal an appearance as possible.

Like any actor who completes a shoot while understanding nothing, I'm tempted to say now, 'I said it from the beginning, I knew it would be good and that it would be a success.'

This is an extract from 'En tournant pour Spielberg' ('Filming for Spielberg'), published in Tony Crawley, *L'Aventure Spielberg*, Pygmalion-Gérard Watelet, Paris, 1984.

Steven Spielberg with François Truffaut on the set of *Close Encounters of the Third Kind* (1977).

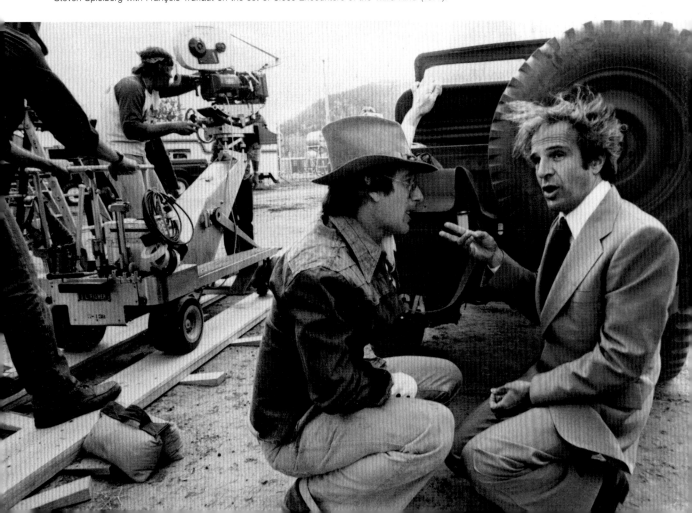

Opposite page and right: *Close Encounters of the Third Kind* (1977).

Following page: Henri Thomas in *E.T.* (1982).

Another point of rupture involves father figures. Richard Dreyfuss behaves like an irresponsible kid, hyperactive and suffocated by the collective hysteria that prevails in his house. He is a man who weeps at the dinner table, whose son calls him a 'cry-baby'. In the end, his obsession with extraterrestrials is no more than a manifestation of a deep depression. The space around him is signposted with American symbols: Shell and McDonald's logos, TV soaps and Budweiser ads, 'Coca-Cola' labelled trucks serving as a cover for the army's planned masquerade. *Close Encounters of the Third Kind* is nothing other than the fugue of a man at odds with America, a deserter who unhesitatingly abandons his family, without showing the least sign of remorse, to board the spaceship at the end of the film. Like its main character, *Close Encounters* is a slightly crazy, unusually diffuse film. It takes us all over the planet, to different countries, in a Babel of languages (including the evocative 'franglais' of the scientist so touchingly played by François Truffaut), following the track of enigmatic clues, an idealistic odyssey, whereas *E.T.* is an 'intimist' adventure centred on a house, a street, a forest. *E.T.* could thus be seen as a sequel to *Close Encounters*: the father has left, the mother is so overwhelmed by daily life and her own unhappiness that she does not notice the intruder living under her roof. Spielberg has never concealed the fact that he sees *E.T.* primarily as a film about his parents' divorce. While the father in *Close Encounters of the Third Kind* invents imaginary friends in order to flee his country and his family, the lonely little boy in *E.T.* invents his friend precisely in order to forget that his father has abandoned him.

E.T. was a phenomenon, breaking every emotional and financial record, and Spielberg touched the world with a kind of mysterious communication that parallels the telepathic relationship between Elliott and E.T. (The second of these names is simply a contraction of the first.) They form a single, indivisible entity, with endlessly thrilling possibilities, as in the brilliant scene in which E.T., watching John Ford's *The Quiet Man*, 'operates' Elliott from a distance so that he re-enacts with a classmate the beautiful windswept kiss between John Wayne and Maureen O'Hara. But soon the intense bond between the child and the extraterrestrial begins to have morbid effects, each of them leading the other towards a death to be shared indiscriminately: 'He's sick. I think we're dying.' Nobody is surprised at Elliott's remark, when we have seen him preparing for Halloween, putting on greenish make-up and painting blood-red rings round his eyes, a little corpse more drawn than one might think by a death-wish. Or when we watch him scream himself hoarse, while no sound comes out of his mouth, paralysed by fear at the first appearance of E.T.

29

Henry Thomas in *E.T.* (1982).

Spielberg and the New Hollywood

From a strictly chronological point of view, Steven Spielberg is part of the 'New Hollywood', that movement in American cinema history that had its roots in the 1960s and that saw changes in the subject matter of films, the way in which they were made and the age of the people making them. During those years of flower power and radical politics, although Spielberg spent a good deal of time at the Malibu home of producers Michael and Julia Phillips, with the group of people who became known as the movie brats – De Palma, Scorsese, Milius, Schrader and the rest – he seemed to be totally out of step with the prevailing culture; he didn't do drugs and was pathologically shy with women; he devoured Hollywood's commercial press and rejected the notion of 'auteur' cinema.

His short film *Amblin'* (1968) was, as he himself admits, made up of an assortment of current fads – road movies, lack of communication, and youthful disillusion: 'It really proved how apathetic I was during the Sixties. When I look back at that film, I can easily say: "No wonder I didn't go to Kent State," or "No wonder I didn't go to Vietnam or I wasn't protesting when all my friends were carrying signs and getting clubbed in Century City." I was off making movies, and *Amblin'* is the slick by-product of a kid immersed up to his nose in film.' (Mitch Tuchman, *Film Comment*, January-February 1978).

From the point of view of their dates and subject-matter, *Duel* and *The Sugarland Express*, two road movies, are potentially his two most 1970s films. But Spielberg 'betrayed' him-self in planning a happy ending for *The Sugarland Express*, to the great displeasure of his producers, who were well aware that audiences of the day were sympathetic towards the tragic destinies of people on the margins, trampled underfoot by society, the model being, of course, *Easy Rider*.

In 1973, Spielberg began to work with Paul Schrader (who would later write the screenplay of *Taxi Driver*) on the script of *Close Encounters of the Third Kind*. But the two of them were forced to admit they were fundamentally incompatible. Spielberg liked ordinary heroes, people from the suburbs. Schrader, with his allergic response to 'Middle America', rejected this idea point-blank : 'If somebody's going to represent me and the human race to get on a spaceship, I don't want my representative to be a guy who eats all his meals at McDonald's,' Schrader yelled at Spielberg. 'That's exactly what I *do* want!' (Peter Biskind, *Easy Riders, Raging Bulls*, London, Bloomsbury, rev. edn, 2009, pp. 262–3). That was the end of their collaboration. Then *Jaws* came out in 1975, inaugurating the blockbusters era, and for a long time Spielberg (with George Lucas, whose *Star Wars* came out two years later) would be seen as the director who sounded the death knell of the first flowering of the New Hollywood. Nevertheless, thirty years later, what do we see on the screen? Extreme, omnipresent violence, a challenge to the authorities, 'guerilla' filming, use of the hand-held camera – all this is in *Munich* (2005). At last, Spielberg had made his only real 1970s film.

Steven Spielberg, Martin Scorsese, Brian De Palma, George Lucas and Francis Ford Coppola celebrate George Lucas's fiftieth birthday in May 1994.

Opposite page and above: *E.T.* (1982).

This dream of a film is often very much like a nightmare, revealing something of the secrets hidden behind the children's bedroom doors, watched over by hideous toys with large red flashing hearts. In a scene that was cut from *Close Encounters*, Truffaut asks his interpreter to translate into English not only the things he says, but also his feelings and emotions. The telepathic communication between the child and his extraterrestrial double is clearly of that order. Here Spielberg is inventing a new kind of sentimentality, which runs the risk of becoming cloying. Yes, it is an enchanting film, 'but it is its moments of disenchantment, or of enchantment carried over into "the light of common day" that make it a great film about childhood.'[9]

Between *Close Encounters of the Third Kind* and *E.T.*, Spielberg made two other films. One was *Raiders of the Lost Ark* (1981), a homage to the Saturday-afternoon adventure films of the 1930s and 1940s. It was followed by two sequels within the decade, and all three were commercial successes. The other, *1941*, made in 1979, was a different story, a big-budget film that ended in a resounding failure. This ironic war comedy, in which the Japanese attack Hollywood, is an explosive super-production that betrays Spielberg's tendency to go over the top. Samuel Fuller, Robert Stack, Christopher Lee and Toshiro Mifune all appear in it, while John Wayne and Charlton Heston refused to take part, because they considered the screenplay too anti-American. The film is tasteless, full of pratfalls, fights, the rattle of submachine gunfire, crashed cars and breaking glass, not to mention juvenile jokes. It is like being in a shopping mall, a toy shop, or a film studio where the brats (John Milius was executive producer, Robert Zemeckis wrote the screenplay[10]) have been shut in for the night. Spielberg picks up his toys and sends them flying around the sets. At this point in his career, the gesture was cheeky and a touch self-assured, in other words, likeable. Spielberg has long felt bad about this failure, but it is just the 'itching-powder' quality of *1941* that supplies its major interest. It is anything but a 'nice' film, showing that those who had put Spielberg's work under that heading were mistaken. With a shockingly precocious debut (*Duel*), a B movie so perfect that it marked the invention of the blockbuster (*Jaws*), two cult films (*Close Encounters of the Third Kind* and *E.T.*), a tribute to the fathers of cinema (*Raiders of the Lost Ark*) and even a flop that was full of panache (*1941*), the first period of Spielberg's career is exemplary.

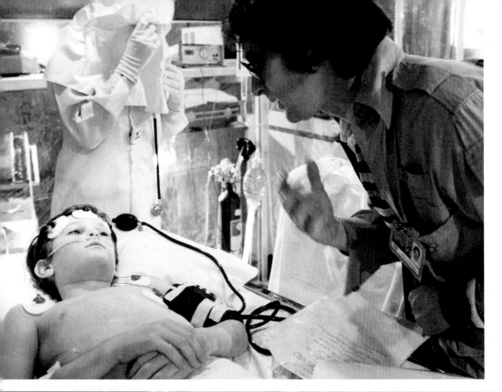

'E.T., the magic frog', by Bill Krohn

Perhaps the best way to get at what is new about the film is to look at the tradition it grows out of. Where does Spielberg come from? From animated cartoons – he has never made a secret of it in his interviews ... The names he most frequently mentions are Walt Disney ('The first film I remember seeing was *Snow White and the Seven Dwarves*') and Chuck Jones, a maverick Disney animator who became the undisputed master of animated slapstick at Warner Bros., where he directed Bugs Bunny and Daffy Duck in some of their best films, and created Wile E. Coyote and the Roadrunner. Jones, whom Spielberg invited to act as 'technical consultant' on *1941*, seems to be the primary influence ... E.T. is a Chuck Jones character living out a Disney scenario – orphaned, adopted, dead and resurrected, rescued at the end – without ever losing his anarchic comic energy, or the touch of mystery that all Jones's 'special' creations share. (The children in the film are also the kind of children – hip and foul-mouthed – that Jones, but certainly not Disney, might have imagined watching his work.) Morphologically, E.T. is distantly related to the Martian character in *Duck Dodgers in the 24½th Century*, who consists of a bowling ball with huge expressive eyes, a spindly body and an oversized pair of tennis shoes, but his nearest ancestor is probably the Magic Frog in Jones's masterpiece, *One Froggy Evening* (1956). In that cartoon, a construction worker who unearths a frog from the cornerstone of a condemned building is startled when the creature breaks into a high-stepping rendition of 'Hello, My Honey' in a voice like Al Jolson's. Sure that his fortune is made, the man rushes to a theatrical agent with his find, but the frog refuses to sing for anyone but him. By the end of the film the man's greed and the frog's obstinate refusal to perform have reduced him to penury and landed him in the madhouse. The ending of *E.T.* is more optimistic. Elliott's first response when he finds his Magic Frog is selfish – 'I'm going to keep him,' he says fervently – but E.T., on the point of death, is able to teach him the necessity of sooner or later letting go ... In Spielberg's hands, Jones's dark fable has become edifying, sentimental; it has been re-Disneyfied, and this does not necessarily imply a criticism. Spielberg's strategy is the strategy of a whole generation, who have created a cinema haunted by modernism (Jones, for example, or Welles) and aspiring to classicism (Disney or, for example, Ford): their Masters' Masters, to put it very schematically.

This is an extract from 'L'été de E.T.', *Cahiers du cinéma*, no. 342, December 1982.

Opposite page, top: Steven Spielberg with Henry Thomas on the set of *E.T.* (1982).

Left: Henry Thomas in *E.T.* (1982).

Right: Chuck Jones's *One Froggy Evening* (1956) and *Duck Dodgers in the 24½th Century* (1953).

Siren Songs

From *Indiana Jones* to *Saving Private Ryan*

Tom Hanks in *Saving Private Ryan* (1998).

What is a man to do if at the age of thirty-six he has already made *E.T.*, the film of his dreams and the film of his life? The period from the beginning of the flashy 1980s to the end of the 1990s was one of both triumph and uncertainty. As head of Amblin Entertainment, the production company he set up in 1982, Spielberg produced some of the decade's most successful American films: Robert Zemeckis's *Back to the Future* trilogy and *Who Framed Roger Rabbit*, and Joe Dante's two *Gremlins* movies.

As a new type of movie mogul, who would actually set up his own studio, DreamWorks, in 1994,[11] the former child prodigy was the object of anything but adulation: he was belittled by his seniors in the industry itself and often mocked, and his films were controversial on various levels. His name on the credits of *The Color Purple* (1985) was seen as unjustified (what did he know about being black?) and the monumental commercial disaster of *Hook* (1991) was greeted with derision. Finally, at the end of this period, there were the debates that followed the release of *Schindler's List* (1993), especially in Europe. Nevertheless, the film earned Spielberg his first Oscar for best director. Success and power of various kinds were thus accompanied by contradictory responses: more than ever, Spielberg celebrated

cinema's younger days (with the Indiana Jones and *Jurassic Park* trilogies), while at the same time demonstrating his fierce determination to grow up, with *The Colour Purple*, *Empire of the Sun* (1987), *Schindler's List* and *Amistad* (1997).

Fathers and sons in Hollywood

It was with George Lucas, his young, all-powerful 'twin brother',[12] that Spielberg conceived the Indiana Jones series. The director of *Jaws* dreamed of making a James Bond movie, but the creator of *Star Wars* persuaded him that together they should develop this new character, a phlegmatic archaeologist—adventurer, dressed in a 'vintage' leather jacket and fedora.[13] This famous hat never blows away and never gets lost, a sign that what we are seeing is really a playfully nostalgic take on the marvellous years of golden-age Hollywood. The Lost Ark, the 'Holy Grail' that Spielberg and Lucas were seeking, was first and foremost the cinema of yesteryear, the adventure films of Michael Curtiz and Raoul Walsh and Humphrey Bogart's ironic smile, which Harrison Ford, blasé and perfectly cast in the role, never fails to imitate. The three films in the series are constructed from the same pattern, an accumulation of closely connected sequences, in a plot that takes off in a new direction every time we think it is reaching a resolution. Objects (gold medallions, plans, the Ark, the Grail — all the gimmicks on which the trilogy is based) pass from hand to hand, crevasses endlessly open up before our eyes, and when we think we are out of danger, the enemy appears out of nowhere and the ally turns traitor in the blink of an eye. With plots constructed like Russian dolls, landslides, and action that is constantly taking sudden new turns, there is an ambush round every corner. Like the booby-trapped terrain that Indiana Jones has to cross, the scene perpetually shifts under your feet, moving like a nest of snakes discovered on the ground when you strike a match. Peopled with mummies and skeletons, and swarming with rats and spiders (all the scary, creepy-crawly horrors that the series indulges in to the hilt), the adventure film according to Spielberg and Lucas is the closest thing to a fairground ghost train (the chase in mine wagons in *Indiana Jones and the Temple of Doom* (1984) follows this motif to the letter). It mixes moments of terror and of false relief, sudden bursts of speed and witty ripostes to the point of extreme exhaustion and not without inducing a certain feeling of vacuousness.

Love, friendship and emotion, not to mention eroticism, have no place in the action, or appear only in 'vignettes', although the erotic is conventionally associated with adventure. In *The Temple of Doom*, Spielberg films Kate Capshaw (who would nonetheless become his wife) as a pathetic, ditzy creature whose shrill screams punctuate the film, like Fay Wray in the original 1933 version of *King Kong*. But Fay Wray's mythic scream, torn dress and ambiguous expression, mingling fear and desire, concealed a potential that Spielberg appears not to see in his female actors. There is something of Tintin about the director: the pure clarity of line and the longstanding total absence of sexuality.[14] Despite its apparent simplicity, this second effort remains the strangest. After the Jewish theme of *Raiders of the Lost Ark* (the Ark of the Covenant) and before the Christian one of *Indiana Jones and the Last Crusade* (1989) (the Holy Grail), *The Temple of Doom* penetrates the white-hot centre of the earth, in pursuit of bloodthirsty pagan rituals in which hearts are torn out with bare hands. Spielberg does not entirely engage with this gory detour through black magic, which was given a PG-13 certificate, something that may seem

Harrison Ford in *Raiders of the Lost Ark* (1981).

contradictory for this eternal child.[15] At this time the 'dark side', so dear to Lucas, was totally alien to Spielberg (or so he still thought, at least).

The nostalgic reference to *King Kong* is not the only echo in these films of a devoted cinephile. Spielberg plays with references to the golden age of Hollywood, starting each film with a version of the Paramount logo, in which the famous studio's painted mountain dissolves into the real landscape, or, in the opening shots of *The Temple of Doom*, appears sculpted in bronze on a gong. We should not forget that the literal meaning of the name Spielberg is 'play mountain' and that the imaginary production company he created as a child was called Playmount. He loves puns (for example, the notorious 'Uranus — your anus' in *E.T.*), and was quite happy to play leisurely games with another mountain, in *Close Encounters of the Third Kind*. In this way, he allows himself the luxury of inscribing his name directly

Kate Capshaw, Steven Spielberg, George Lucas and Harrison Ford on the set of *Indiana Jones and the Temple of Doom* (1984).

in the annals of a legendary studio, whereas other directors are content with a star on the pavement of Hollywood Boulevard. He also makes brief allusions to the great film genres: *The Temple of Doom* opens with a brilliant sequence in red and gold, evoking scenes from Vincente Minnelli's musical, *Ziegfeld Follies* (1945). *The Last Crusade* is framed by a prologue and epilogue in the style of a western, and ends with a shot of three horsemen riding off into the sunset, but this time in the Jordanian desert. The closing shot of *Raiders of the Lost Ark*, in which the Ark of the Covenant, recovered at last, is put into storage in a warehouse full of identical crates, emphasizing that the film 'has no point', is a direct reference to the end of *Citizen Kane* (1941).[16]

When, twenty years later, Spielberg returned to his hero in the soft hat for a fourth adventure (*Indiana Jones and the Kingdom of the Crystal Skull*, 2008), he decided to open with a scene set in an

43

Spielberg's actors

Richard Dreyfuss, the alter ego
Spielberg cast Richard Dreyfuss three times in the 1970s and 1980s: in *Jaws*, *Close Encounters of the Third Kind* and *Always*. For him, Dreyfuss represented the average American. He has said that he saw in the actor from *American Graffiti* a possible contemporary reincarnation of Spencer Tracy, his favourite actor: 'It's easier to identify with Richard than with, let's say, Robert Redford. I've always had the feeling that in my films, the principal character ought to be – and probably always will be – an Everyman figure.'

Harrison Ford, the fantasy figure
But Spielberg was mistaken. Very soon, with growing success, and commanding ever more colossal budgets, he started dreaming about a hero, a real one: he would be Indiana Jones, adventurer and archaeologist, and therefore both muscular and intelligent. To play him, Spielberg chose Harrison Ford, the intergalactic hero of *Star Wars*, sexy and athletic, always happy to treat a woman roughly, with an insincerely apologetic smile on his lips. In short, a modern, slightly disillusioned, Kirk Douglas.

The two Toms:
Hanks versus Cruise
Things became more complicated in the most recent period. In Tom Hanks, Spielberg found the perfect embodiment of the average man, an heir to James Stewart. But in *Saving Private Ryan*, his character, an elementary school teacher from the Midwest, proved to be a war hero; in *The Terminal*, he played the hero living in an airport concourse, where the image of his hand, as a symbol of resistance, was displayed everywhere on posters. Tom Cruise, on the other hand, a depressed cop in *Minority Report* and a docker and bad father in *War of the Worlds*, was relegated by Spielberg from superstar to human being. The inversion of the two great figures by Spielberg was complete: the ordinary man had become a hero despite himself, and the star had turned into Everyman.

From left to right:
Tom Hanks in *Saving Private Ryan* (1998),
Harrison Ford in *Indiana Jones and the Last Crusade* (1989),
Richard Dreyfuss in *Close Encounters of the Third Kind* (1977),
Tom Cruise in *Minority Report* (2002).

Richard Dreyfuss, Holly Hunter and Brad Johnson in *Always* (1989).

identical warehouse, in which all the world's treasure lay sleeping. It was another visit to this quintessential setting, and reinforced the relationship of the series with films of the past. After 2006, when action films were changing fast (from Christian Bale's neurasthenic Batman, in Christopher Nolan's *Batman Begins*, to the rapid-fire editing of the action scenes in the Jason Bourne films), Spielberg cannily decided not to update the way he filmed the character, and defended his 'old-fashioned' approach. Nonetheless, at the end of this film, Indy's hat does blow away, rolling towards his son's feet. But Harrison Ford catches it, and rams it back on his head with a defiant little smile; that gesture, a refusal to pass on the torch, is the last shot of the film. In other words, films of this kind are our fathers' affair.

These repeated tributes to the films of a previous generation found their natural culmination in 1989, in *Always*, which Spielberg made immediately after the third Indiana Jones film. It was a remake of Victor Fleming's *A Guy Named Joe* (1943), which starred Spencer Tracy, the perfect father-figure for the young Steven. A dead aviator comes back to earth to train a young pilot, who is unaware of his identity, and to help him find love with the grieving partner he has left behind (played here by Holly Hunter). The role was taken by Richard Dreyfuss, the 'alter ego' of Spielberg's early films. The *mise en scène* is deliberately 'retro', with old World War II planes and 1950s classic tunes, but the plot is contemporary. It is a curious, slightly sugary film, balanced on a knife-edge, a back-to-front tear-jerker (the hero 'dies' at the beginning) held together by a few notes of a song performed by the Platters, 'Smoke Gets In Your Eyes', and especially by a strange piece of magic that Spielberg explains in his own way; namely, that just like Richard Dreyfuss, sitting in the cockpit behind his replacement and whispering

Whoopi Goldberg in *The Color Purple* (1985).

instructions to him, the ghosts of the Hollywood old-timers, Capra, Fleming, Sturges and the rest, are there, behind his shoulder, whispering a few of their timeless secrets in his ear.

Growing up

Spielberg was a young man in the 1970s and had watched with cool detachment the rise of protest and the counterculture. But having been a small Jewish boy in a predominantly Christian environment, he was extraordinarily sensitive to discrimination, and became impassioned about a single movement — Civil Rights. 'Steven and I, we wanted to be black', recalls a friend from their teenage years, who shared Spielberg's emotional commitment to the black struggle, and who, as Joseph McBride said, was probably the only person not to be surprised to learn that he was about to adapt Alice Walker's bestseller, *The Color Purple*. But empathy does not necessarily

make for good films. With the intention of making his first 'serious' film, Spielberg actually made his first academic film. *Amistad*, his pretentious epic on the subject of slavery, made twelve years later, would suffer from the same defects. *The Color Purple*, a saga weighed down with glowing red sunsets and milky lighting effects, focuses on the sacrificial figure of its principal character, Celie, a child victim of rape, an abused wife and a mother robbed of her children, while on its periphery is Shug, a lively and penniless jazz singer who provides a perfect blues element. The film's best moments are the scenes in which she sings, including one reminiscent of John Ford, which moves from a bar to a church, from blues to gospel music. It makes us wonder briefly whether *The Color Purple* is perhaps not an unsuccessful film for adults but a musical comedy manqué.

Hook raises the opposite problem. Here it is not a matter of emerging from childhood, but of

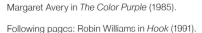

Margaret Avery in *The Color Purple* (1985).

Following pages: Robin Williams in *Hook* (1991).

putting it behind one by plunging into it again (one almost wants to say by gorging oneself on it, the film is so indigestible) one last time. With *Hook*, the Spielberg system came up against its furthest limit. The screenplay takes up the story of Peter Pan, the famous 'boy who wouldn't grow up', a description that perfectly fits the director of *E.T.*, who nevertheless went horribly astray here. The disaster was as much aesthetic as commercial. *Hook* proves to be a film about hating children (a sentiment shared by Sam Neill's character in *Jurassic Park*, who declares, 'They're stinky'). Peter, now an overworked corporate lawyer, has acquired the features of Robin Williams. He has put his childhood behind him and disowned his very serious fantasies. When his daughter asks him to smell a paper flower she has made, he replies coldly, 'It's just paper.' Everything about *Hook* exudes this feeling of disgust, starting with Neverland, a crude Disneyland inhabited by brats on skateboards, daubed with face-paint. Bidden to return to the land of his rejected childhood, Robin Williams does his utmost to rejuvenate himself, decked out in a ridiculous wig. The attempt fails, although, in a slightly worrying coincidence, in 1996 Francis Ford Coppola hired Williams for the title role in *Jack*, playing a ten-year-old child with a degenerative disease that makes him age four times as fast as normal, so that he looks like a man of forty. Between, Spielberg's adult reluctantly trapped in the body of an old kid in make-up, and Coppola's child, whose spirit is trapped in an ageing body bound to die soon, the second is, needless to say, the darker and the more convincing. What Spielberg misses in *Hook* is the way children grow up too quickly, perhaps because he had already filmed it a few years previously in *Empire of the Sun* (1987), a little-known gem from that period.

That is because, in order to become a grown-up director, he had to film a real child. The child in *Empire of the Sun*, based on J. G. Ballard's auto-biographical novel, is highly unusual: an incurable chatterbox, cheeky and always bubbling over with excitement, James Graham (aged eleven when the film begins) declares he is an atheist, says he is going to write a book on bridge and, obsessed with planes, wants to join the Japanese airforce, a heretical notion for a young English boy who has been living in a peaceful international enclave in a residential district of Shanghai, during the Sino-Japanese war. In 1941 he becomes separated from his parents just as the Japanese army enters the city, ending up in a prisoner-of-war camp (since Japan is now also at war with the Allies). The film follows the four lonely but adventure-filled years that this lost, hyper-imaginative boy spends there. Moments of deferment, poetic chaos, every possible effect is exploited to recreate the visions of a whimsical child in a troubled time, such as the dazzling flash of light that Jamie takes to be the soul of the dead woman over whose body he is keeping watch, before he learns that it was the atomic bomb explosion at Hiroshima. For all his atheism, Jamie is also a mystic.

No doubt because he sees something familiar in him, Spielberg delights in recreating the wild imaginings of his young hero, a precocious stager of his own adventures. Endowed with a pronounced taste for bravura, Jamie plants himself in front of the Japanese tanks, saying solemnly, 'I surrender!', or invents for himself an impossible piece of slow motion, when an American bomber flies past, almost level with the ground, and the pilot waves to him. The film's epic form is both blown apart and enriched by this feverish, manic figure, played by the very impressive Christian Bale, in whom Spielberg seems to have found something of Jean-Pierre Léaud in *The 400 Blows* (1959): the same distress turned into energy, the same heart-breaking loneliness.

Right, top: *Freedom From Fear*
(1943), a painting by Norman
Rockwell.

Right, bottom: *Empire of the Sun*
(1987).

Opposite page, top:
Jean-Pierre Léaud in François
Truffaut's *The 400 Blows* (1959).

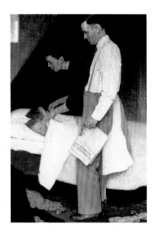

Christian Bale in *Empire of the Sun* (1987).

Jamie's complex relationship with Basie, the rather unsuitable adoptive father that he has chosen for himself, a Dickensian rascal (played by John Malkovich), who picks him up and discards him at his own convenience, is at the heart of the film. Jamie manages, with great difficulty, to get on the lorry leaving for the camp, after Basie, deaf to his cries for help, has knocked him out. He is bleeding from the forehead: in his rage, he did not feel the wound he sustained while climbing on board. It is an irreparable act of abandonment, the end of innocence, and it takes place, almost without our noticing it, in a single scene. The film's inspired lyricism serves only to soften a little the pain of this childhood prematurely snatched away, and the blood running down Jamie's forehead is one of its signifiers. The other is the Norman Rockwell picture[17] from which Jamie is never separated, a sentimental image of family life in which two idealized parents are tucking their

children into bed. Like a freeze-frame from a bygone era, the picture ends up in the suitcase abandoned by Jamie, who is drifting aimlessly, like the floating graves we saw in the first shot of the film, the ultimate sign of what has died inside him while he has been doing all he can not to allow himself to die.

Elements of *Empire of the Sun* infiltrate all Spielberg's later work: the image of the graves on the water reappears, in a more radical form, with the corpses swept down the river in *War of the Worlds*, a film that more generally takes up the motif of a subjective apocalypse seen through the eyes of a single being. The adventure of an unconventional, abandoned small boy is also the subject of *A.I.* The prisoner-of-war camp, with its huge gates opening onto the railway lines, as well as the images of the exodus of the defeated crowd, prefigures *Schindler's List*. And the surrealistic stadium full of the possessions — chandeliers, cars, statues — seized by the

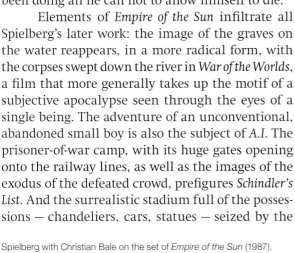

Spielberg with Christian Bale on the set of *Empire of the Sun* (1987).

Left: Steven Spielberg with producer Kathleen Kennedy on the set of *Jurassic Park* (1993).

Below: *Jurassic Park* (1993).

Pages 56–7: Laura Dern, Jeff Goldblum and Bob Peck in *Jurassic Park* (1993).

Page 58–9: Joseph Mazzello and Ariana Richards in *Jurassic Park* (1993).

Pop Art

Spielberg's vision of America is inextricably bound up with the imagery of advertising. He grew up in the suburbs, and to his eye, these quintessential, immediately identifiable images are scattered all over the American landscape, coloured neon signs lighting up the outskirts of cities. In *Close Encounters of the Third Kind*, when a power cut plunges a whole state into darkness, the McDonald's sign and the Shell logo are the first things to go out.

This sensitivity to the visual landscape of trademarks sometimes holds a meaning: in the same film, the army, who want to conceal the imminent arrival of the extraterrestrials from the American public, camouflage their trucks with travelling advertisements for Coca-Cola, Baskin-Robbins ice-cream or the laughing piglet of Piggly Wiggly supermarkets, all familiar, nostalgic logos, designed to lull the population's suspicions. Spielberg's first design for the

spaceship in *Close Encounters of the Third Kind* was actually a variation on the McDonald's sign: the extraterrestrials, having noticed how many of these luminous yellow signs there were on the American continent, had designed their two vessels to give earthlings an instantly reassuring image. Each UFO was to have been in the shape of an arch so that, when they came together, they would overlap to form a slightly irregular version of the hamburger giant's

rounded 'M'. There are many other examples: E.T. gets drunk on Coors beer, and in *The Lost World*, the big red ball emblazoned with the number 76, the symbol of a famous chain of petrol stations, plays an active part in the plot, pulled down by *Tyrannosaurus rex* and hurled into the city streets. As in the work of Andy Warhol and other exponents of Pop Art, advertising images are often used in Spielberg's films to create an aesthetic environment.

Above, left: *The Lost World* (1997).   Above, right: detail of Andy Warhol's *Campbell's Soup Cans* (1968).

Japanese clearly evokes the pillage of Jewish property by the Nazis. It is also the 'burial ground' in which Spielberg is beginning to deposit the remains of a type of cinema he has gradually been preparing to leave behind. *Empire of the Sun* stands at the crossroads between fantasized views of children's dreams and the destruction of those same dreams, a strange blend of excitement and disillusion. It marks the hidden transition between the two halves of Spielberg's career, a transition that will ultimately be confirmed by *Schindler's List*, of course, but also, in a less obvious way, by the two *Jurassic Park* films.

No Trespassing

When he smashed his own box-office records with *Jurassic Park* in 1993 (and its sequel, *The Lost World*, in 1997), for many film-goers Spielberg had long been the embodiment of the cynical movie

entrepreneur, the director who invented 'product placement' with the multicoloured 'Reese's Pieces' sweets that feature prominently in *E.T.* There's an additional twist here: the mugs, caps and other souvenir items stamped with the words 'Jurassic Park' that are noticed by the scientists who are the first visitors to the park, in the film, are exactly the same as those that inundated the planet when the film came out. The logo is the same inside (on the signage of the park) and outside (on the film posters) for this film, which actually incorporates the products it generates, attacking them in fiction but profiting from them in reality. What could be better than to admit one's own megalomania while at the same time pocketing the rewards?

What the two *Jurassic Park* movies begin to question, while at the same time attaining new heights of technical perfection, is the status of

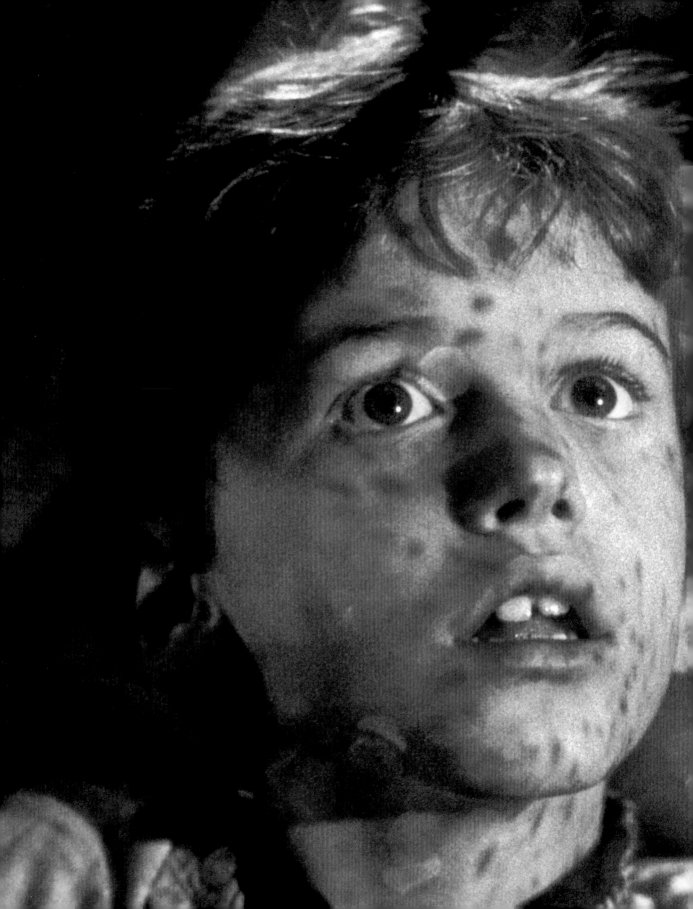

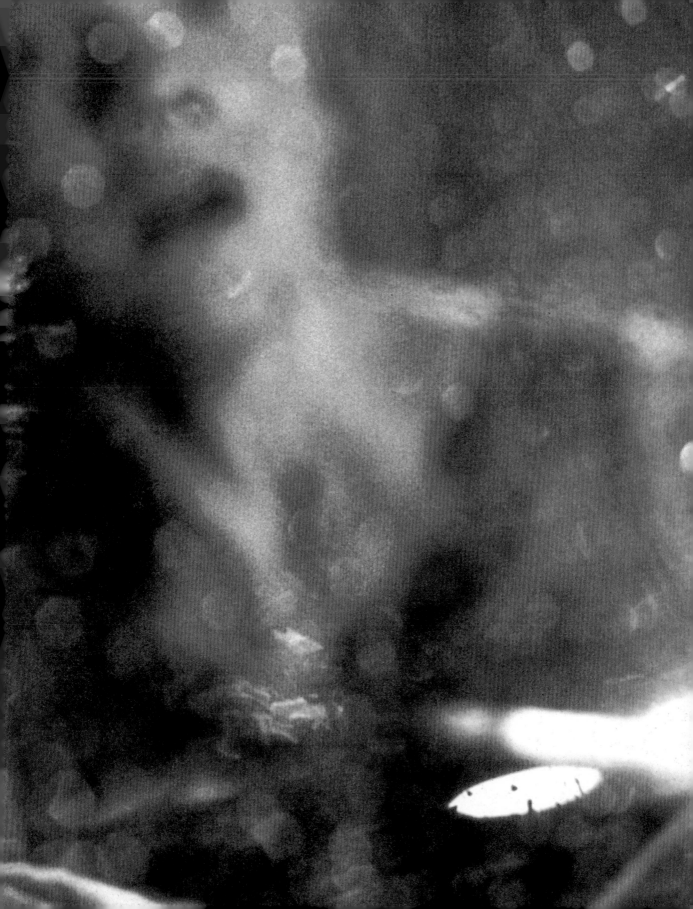

American cinema as an amusement park. Digital images make so much possible that we will never again ask, 'How did they do that?' Cooper and Schoedsack's version of *King Kong*, a constant reference point for the two films (the island, the door, the very theme of *The Lost World*, from which *Tyrannosaurus rex* is brought back to America to be put on display), has already been left far behind. The park's designer, played by Richard Attenborough, describes how he started out with a fairground flea circus. Starting from home-made illusionistic effects, Méliès-style, and proceeding by way of *King Kong* to the contemporary blockbuster, Spielberg swept through the entire history of entertainment cinema before double-locking behind him the gates of this modern-day Xanadu (*Citizen Kane*, again).

If *Jurassic Park* presents us with horror in broad daylight, *The Lost World* offers ever darker tones, damp, rainy settings and unrelieved desolation. It is full of the ruins left behind in the first film, down to the tracking shot that travels from an abandoned man-made metal structure to a series of giant dinosaur bones, the two linked together by their common obsolescence. The mechanical shark of *Jaws* and the ghost train of *Indiana Jones and the Temple of Doom* have now been overtaken by virtual creations of unmitigated cruelty, 'descendants of *Alien* and not of *Bambi*. Vicious, inhuman killing machines ... *Jurassic Park* describes the end of the world, literally, not metaphorically. Or more specifically, the end of a (personal?) cycle, as if Spielberg was trying to tell us he no longer had the heart to laugh.'[18] There is a troubling parallel: we would swear, would we not, that this quotation is referring to *War of the Worlds*, made twelve years later?[19]

Schindler's List

Sid Sheinberg, Spielberg's mentor from the start, had bought the film rights of Thomas Keneally's book as early as 1982. For ten years, Spielberg waited, drew back, hesitated. He finally began shooting *Schindler's List* in between the two *Jurassic Park* films, a chronological arrangement that is surprising and perhaps even shocking. But it is part of a long tradition among Hollywood directors to alternate commercial films and more personal works, the famous principle of 'one for them, one for me'. This is complicated in Spielberg's case, since 'them' is, in fact, also himself and his insatiable thirst for success.

Schindler's List (1993).

This typically Spielbergian paradox continued while *Schindler's List* was being made (on some evenings during filming in Poland, Spielberg would check progress on post-production of the dinosaurs in California), and it recurs in the complex and ambiguous figure of the real-life Oskar Schindler, a member of the Nazi party, a bon vivant, a happy-go-lucky womanizer and wheeler-dealer who gradually finds himself nagged by his conscience into action. Schindler begins by taking Jews from the Płaszów forced-labour camp out of pure self-interest, in order to keep his factory running, and ends by doing so in order to save their lives. Spielberg, a person and a filmmaker who is both cynical and sentimental, clearly found in this intriguing life-

Following pages: Ralph Fiennes and Liam Neeson in *Schindler's List* (1993).

story the material for a self-portrait 'at one remove'. Making this film also led to a degree of personal involvement that was crucial for him. By filming a small part of the indescribable tragedy suffered by the Jewish people, he exposed for the first time in his career (and his life) a Jewishness that had hitherto been problematical for him. A man who, as a child, would simply ignore his grandfather when he addressed him by his religious name ('Shmuel! Shmuel!') in front of his non-Jewish friends, decided to make *Schindler's List*, and then to set up the Shoah Foundation. At the age of almost fifty, Spielberg was finally answering his grandfather.

For the first time, he used the services of the cinematographer Janusz Kaminski, a Pole who had settled in Hollywood. Together, they decided to make the film in black and white, and to use, for the most part, a shaky, sensitive hand-held camera.[20] The cinematography of *Schindler's List* is raw and sharp, as never before in Spielberg's work. Like the black-on-white names on the list to which the title refers, the black-and-white images of the destruction of the Kraków ghetto, or the final selection of old men for Auschwitz, captured by an appalled news camera, imprint themselves on the *memory*, because that is what it is about.

'All sorrows can be endured if they're turned into a story or if you tell a story about them.' The words are Karen Blixen's, used later by the philosopher Hannah Arendt.[21] By choosing a subject that

Ralph Fiennes, Ben Kingsley, Steven Spielberg and Liam Neeson on the set of *Schindler's List* (1993).

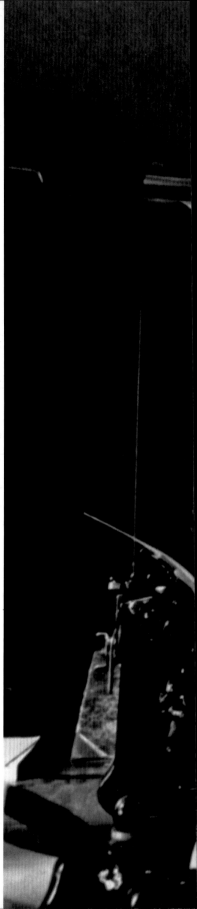

is on the 'edge' of what cannot be represented (the Płaszów camp was not an extermination camp, but first a forced-labour camp, then from 1944 a concentration camp, with the accelerated thrust towards the 'final solution'), Spielberg stops at the threshold of absolute horror, at a point where it is still possible to tell a story.[22] In any case, he did not have permission to shoot the famous shower scene at Auschwitz, and was allowed to film only the gates of the camp. The scene in question is highly problematic: the group of women sent to Auschwitz by mistake, when Schindler had arranged for them to go to his factory in Czechoslovakia, find themselves in the showers. After a few minutes of unbearable suspense for the viewer, it is water that is seen coming out of the shower-heads. Although it is based on a real incident, the sequence introduces a form of suspense, of purely cinematic effectiveness, which is unthinkable here.

Liam Neeson and Ben Kingsley in Schindler's List (1993).

For this one moment the film crosses the threshold and ventures into the realm of the unrepresentable, and finds its limits there: just as Spielberg cannot recreate an extermination camp, he cannot make anything but water come out of shower-heads. Under our eyes *Schindler* thus stumbles over its own inability to take a story to its furthest point, and the film contains an admission of this fact, just like the list itself, which is structurally limiting. 'Schindler's Jews', who numbered 1,100, and who were returned to life at the very last moment, suggest (by their absence) the six million who did not return, like the little girl whose coat is shown in colour, a metonymic device for the colour of blood. Each shot has its unbearable 'off-screen' counterpart, unbearable due to the numbers involved. In this way *Schindler's List* is constructed around what is missing, as much as around what it shows. And that is why this impossible, necessarily imperfect film nevertheless remains an important one.

Afflicted by the same fever as Schindler, Spielberg nevertheless did his best to stretch the list to the maximum. The return to colour in the film's final images and the long procession of 'Schindler's Jews' (all accompanied by the actors who play them in the film) past his grave in Jerusalem are hints about what will be the great project of the next few years: the creation of the Survivors of the Shoah Visual History Foundation, an organization whose task will be to collect, on film, from every country, the living words of those who survived the Shoah. Fifty-two thousand testimonies are currently available in the Foundation's databank.

Tom Hanks in *Saving Private Ryan* (1998).

Memory has lost its purchase
A name that has no more flesh than a number
A toneless voice that sings
In the void where words dissolve
The snow can no longer rise nor fall
Since there is no more down nor up
And in this future heavy as a lampless night
No wave of a hand
No rustle of a wing
Nothing
Not even an echo [23]

After *The Lost World* and the unmemorable *Amistad* (both 1997), Spielberg ended the decade with a real war film, his first. *Saving Private Ryan* is an impressive reconstruction of the Normandy landings of June 1944 and the wanderings of a handful of soldiers through the French countryside in search of Private Ryan. The film describes an absurd quest, reminiscent of Samuel Beckett; it is disorientating, clever and misleading, full of false leads — the close-up of the eyes of the old man who starts the flashback at the beginning takes us back, for example, to a moment when this character (as we will only later learn) is not there.

As is often the case in good war films, *Saving Private Ryan* owes much to its scenes of suspended action, inactivity, waiting. Or of astonishment, as when the unit finds itself in a small village in

the Normandy countryside and a father, in panic, entrusts his daughter to one of them. Fighting breaks out against the Germans positioned at the other end of the village. When things have calmed down, the American hands the little girl back to the Frenchman, and she repeatedly slaps her father, coldly, saying over and over, 'What'd you do that for?' mechanically, like a cracked record. That is what *Saving Private Ryan* is like: unpredictable, slightly surreal, while at the same time extremely realistic (the bullets whistling past our ears, the taste of dried blood), as beautiful as the anger of a little girl in a ruined village.Had it come out five years later, *Private Ryan* would probably have been seen, not as a great subject, but as a true conceptual film. But the fact is that the previous fifteen years had been uneven, almost confused, with costly box-office mistakes (*Hook*), the treacherous temptations of 'academicism' (*The Color Purple*, *Amistad*), the loss of innocence (*Empire of the Sun*, *Schindler's List*), and the liberation that comes from it. Spielberg had taken cinema-as-amusement-park to its farthest point, and had lost interest in it at exactly the same time (with the *Jurassic Park* films). In short, some films were orientated towards the future, while others still looked back at an ossified past, a constant movement back and forth, a storm in a director's brain: it was, clearly, fascinating to watch.

Revelation

From *Artificial Intelligence: A.I.* to *Munich*

'The loveliest things in life, Tom, are but shadows.'
Charles Dickens (*Martin Chuzzlewit*, 1844)

Tom Cruise in *War of the Worlds* (2005).

The lost children

After devoting almost fifteen years to historical films or films set in the past (of eleven, only four — *Always*, *Hook* and the two *Jurassic Park* movies — had a contemporary setting, but only just …), Spielberg opened the new century with two futuristic works: *Artificial Intelligence: A.I.* and *Minority Report* (2002). With *A.I.*, a small tremor went through (mainly European) critical and cinephile circles, which had not felt the hesitant but perceptible micro-shocks of the preceding period; was this really Spielberg, this puzzling, raw and almost stridently painful film? It did not seem possible.

People were disconcerted, and after *A.I.* opened there was much talk of the influence of Stanley Kubrick, who had long entertained thoughts of making the film before he passed the project over to Spielberg. But hindsight, and the works that followed, confirmed on the contrary how much *A.I.* was an eminently personal undertaking for Spielberg, and at the same time a reformulation of the kind of film he had always known how to make. A first sign of this was that his name appeared in the title credits as screenwriter, something that had not happened since *Close Encounters of the Third Kind*, almost twenty years previously.

The second clue was the way *A.I.*'s strange visual quality, its occasional ugliness, pushed even further the changes in style that had suggested themselves in *Schindler's List* and *Saving Private Ryan*. It was as if, in an attempt to make a definitive break with the period look of *The Color Purple* and the artificiality of *Hook*, Spielberg felt it necessary to test the limits one last time. The garish kitsch of *A.I.*, the sequences at the Flesh Fair (a show where robots due to be scrapped are thrown on the mercy of the public in an act of apocalyptic savagery close to the aesthetic of *Mad Max*) and in Rouge City (a Disneyland of debauchery) carry the mark of this radical purpose and make *A.I.* a film that is difficult to love at first. This works rather well, since its theme is precisely the desperate search for love, told in the form of a ramshackle story, by a child who is difficult to love.

David (Haley Joel Osment), a latest-generation robot, is the perfect child: always happy, never ill, and above all, thanks to some revolutionary technology, capable of love. Placed with a couple whose biological son is in an induced coma, David is a toy for grown-ups. All they have to do, if they decide to adopt him after having him at home for a few days, is to use a code to activate his eternal,

Right: Haley Joel Osment in
Artificial Intelligence: A.I. (2001).

Opposite page, top: Steven
Spielberg with Jude Law and Haley
Joel Osment on the set of
Artificial Intelligence: A.I. (2001).

Opposite page, bottom:
Haley Joel Osment in *Artificial
Intelligence: A.I.* (2001).

unconditional affection. This irreversible action, which the mother performs almost for want of anything better to do, creates in the child-robot a thirst for emotional certainty that he will have to set against the world's unfair harshness in such matters. 'His love is real, but he is not' was one of the lines with which the film was advertised. It is also the tragedy of Spielberg's modern-day Pinocchio.

'I like your floor' is the first sentence this decidedly odd child (in this respect a distant cousin of Jamie in *Empire of the Sun*) utters when he arrives at the couple's home. There follows a series of queasy 'gaffes' (as when he surprises his mother in the toilet, thinking she is playing hide-and-seek), blank reactions and terrifying, dispro-portionate laughter: the mechanical applied to the mechanical (here Bergson's formula is radically altered).[24] Haley Joel Osment clearly uses his own already frightening status as a precocious child actor (first revealed in M. Night Shyamalan's *Sixth Sense* in 1999) to give life to the slightly waxy face, the unblinking eyes and out-of-sync gestures of this alien being. The film is a double self-por-trait, of Haley Joel Osment and of Spielberg him-self, whose own mother saw him as a monster: 'When he was growing up, I didn't know he was a genius. Frankly, I didn't know what the hell he was. You see, Steven wasn't exactly cuddly. What he was was scary. When Steven woke up from a nap, I shook.'[25]

All the embarrassing gestures of the machine-child (Elliott and E.T. finally fused together) are thus left in suspense, in a dramatic gradation: first, an outstretched hand that the mother does not take, then the same hand, reaching up from the bottom of the swimming pool where the adults have left him, to the heart-breaking scene in which he is abandoned in the forest, an astonished little figure, diminishing in the rear-view mirror. David then embarks on an odyssey divided into scenes, in search of Pinocchio's Blue Fairy, the one who could turn him into a 'real' little boy. This quest through the forests and the 'red cities' even takes him under the sea, in a superb sequence in which he dives into the water that has engulfed New York City and passes through the gates of a drowned Coney Island fair-ground, where we can still read, under all the sea-weed and decomposition, the words 'Once upon a time…'. It is Spielberg's farewell to fairy stories.

The film's happy epilogue, a final day that David spends with his mother, who has miracu-lously become loving, is as illusory as it is tragic. The real ending had come with David gazing for ever into the eyes of the tinselly Blue Fairy, at the bottom of the ocean. This false, honey-coloured ending contains the last remnants of Spielberg's old aesthetic. There will be no more of that warm, maternal, broody feeling. With this first inadequate mother (and she will not be the last), a light has gone out in Spielberg's work.

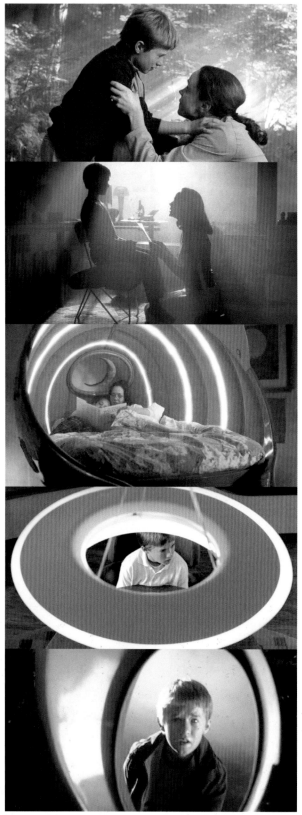

The light and the circle

Opposite page, left column:
E.T. (1982); right column: *Artificial Intelligence: A.I.* (2001).

Below: Steven Spielberg on the set of *Indiana Jones and the Last Crusade* (1989).

E.T. / A.I.: two pairs of initials that mean more or less the same thing (extraterrestrial/artificial intelligence), a child looking for a surrogate father, and another child trying to win the love of an adoptive mother. In the first film, Spielberg sets up his 'system'; in the second he deconstructs it by repeating the same motifs. Twenty years have passed between the two.

First, there is a small boy, seen from behind, facing a stream of bright light, the magical, quasi-divine radiance of the imagination: it is the Spielbergian image *par excellence*, and also appears in *Close Encounters of the Third Kind*. Some years later, the divine rays are segmented by the trees of the forest, in which the mother is about to abandon her child. The forest is a primordial element in *E.T.*; it is where E.T. first appears, a place where children play. In *A.I.*, it has become a place of perdition.

Two face-to-face encounters: that of Elliott and E.T. and that of the mother and David. Otherness has been transferred. It is the child who is now the alien. Light, which was a protective halo in *E.T.*, is more solemn, almost funereal, in *A.I.*

Then, there are two mothers, each of whom relates a story: *Peter Pan* in *E.T.*, *Pinocchio* in *A.I.*, neither of which is without effect. In *A.I.*, the young woman is lying in encircling warmth beside her biological child, while David is excluded from it, all alone in a corner of the bedroom, off-screen. And we should not forget that for Spielberg, both the circle and roundness are maternal, comforting: the spaceship in *E.T.* is completely round, and the one in *Close Encounters of the Third Kind* was rounded on one side, like a giant breast.

In *E.T.*, the circle is divided equally between Elliott and E.T.; it moves to surround each of them in turn, and to unite them for ever. In *A.I.*, like a scratched record, it is always the same being who finds himself trapped in a circle that has become a prison: first, at table, separated from the parents in the shot, then in the rear-view mirror, with the incredulous look of someone who is being left behind.

Like a haunting obsession, the lost child and the swimming pool surface again in *Minority Report*, this time literally, when Tom Cruise, coming out of the pool where he was having an underwater breath-holding contest with his son, realizes that the boy has disappeared from the poolside. He lost sight of him for a moment and now he has lost him forever, such is the dead-zone, the impossible flash-back that serves as the background for a film (its director's most 'theoretical' one) entirely governed by the ideas of sight and vision: the eye and the image, what is shown, but also, above all, what is hidden.

Based on a short story by Philip K. Dick, *Minority Report* is set in 2054 and is about an experimental FBI unit whose task is to prevent crimes before they are committed, using the predictions that three 'precogs' (teenagers kept in a trance-state in a kind of amniotic fluid) project onto a screen above their heads. Tom Cruise's job is therefore to arrest the 'pre-guilty'. This futuristic film explores the limits of surveillance in a society that is about to trample on the idea of the presumption of innocence. Such was the far-from-innocent subject with which Spielberg chose to address the immediate post-9/11 situation.

It is a brilliant exercise, and *Minority Report* soon turns science fiction into a multiplicity of projections: images are projected everywhere, from the walls of shopping malls to the characters' sick minds. The visions of the precogs do not have the square corners of a cinema screen; their shape, like an iris ringed with black, is reminiscent of images from the early days of cinema. The countless projections on glass that occur throughout the film inevitably reminds us of animated daguerreotypes in which the dead, spectral images appear still to move. The homages to film noir — Tom Cruise, a

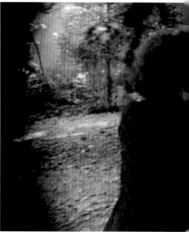

Opposite page, left: Tom Cruise in *Minority Report* (2002).

Centre, top and bottom: *Minority Report* (2002).

Above: Steven Spielberg with Tom Cruise and Samantha Morton on the set of *Minority Report* (2002).

weary Philip Marlowe, watching Samuel Fuller's *House of Bamboo* (1955), or the final slip of the tongue by the bad guy, a reference to Fritz Lang's *Beyond a Reasonable Doubt* (1956)[26] — only underline it; this disillusioned film on the deceptive nature of images carries within itself a nostalgia for new beginnings, while the images themselves still fill us with wonder. A new Spielbergian conviction arrives with *Minority Report*: images are a snare and a delusion,[27] and bound to be suspect. We have therefore to study them, like a piece of exposed flesh, as in the superb opening sequence in which Tom Cruise searches the 'crime scene' projected on a glass screen, raising his hands like an orchestral conductor and using an imaginary focusing wheel to move forwards or back. But this moving flesh is nonetheless frozen, an organism that has been bled dry, like the unsaturated colours of the film. The 3D home movies that Cruise watches nostalgically

in his apartment show him his wife and son, real when seen full-face, but mere ghostly droplets that disappear as soon as he turns them around. When the image has been compromised, all that remains is the seeing eye; the question, 'Can you see?', which the precog Agatha (Samantha Morton) repeatedly asks Tom Cruise, might suggest hope, but the only possible answer offered by Cruise, a masochistic star, is enucleation, pure and simple. His eyes are removed and then replaced, but it is still the same sights that he sees.

The early 2000s thus found Spielberg both liberated and sceptical, more open than ever to experimentation: 'Right now in my life I'm in a period where I'm experimenting, where I'm trying things that challenge me. And as I challenge myself, I also challenge the audience. Now I feel that I'm striking out in all directions trying to find myself, trying to discover myself. In my mid-fifties!'[28]

Literally and (dis)figuratively

Artificial Intelligence: A.I. and *Minority Report*: two consecutive films in which Spielberg experiments, plays with reflections, distorts the image. The first victims of this distortion are the faces of his characters. Through a pane of patterned glass, the face of little David in *A.I.* is seen at first slashed, cut into sharp slices. Then a fault in his circuitry causes it to sag horribly, returning him to his tragic condition as a robot. Later, when he has reached the end of his journey, David sees the Blue Fairy through the window of his amphibious vessel: their faces are superimposed and bleed into one another. The child's drooping eyes distort the statue's perfect almonds; one's gaping mouth and the other's floating smile together form a strange mobile portrait. When David tries to touch his dream, he hugs her a little too hard. The dream also has a face, which then breaks into a thousand pieces.

In *Minority Report*, Tom Cruise watches himself on the screen. So far, nothing out of the ordinary, it happens every day when you are a star. But in this case, it is to discover that he is a killer. In *A.I.*, it was two different faces that were blended together, those of the child and the fairy. Here, Cruise is superimposed on himself, like a kind of Jekyll and Hyde. The effect it produces is terrifying, and prefigures the next step, an exact repetition of what happened to David in *A.I.* – one side of his face droops like melting wax, and yet Tom Cruise is not (in the film) a robot. The impulse to deform has been taken to extremes, with the involvement of a co-operative actor for whom this is not a first attempt, given his mutilated cheek in John Woo's *M:I-2* (2000), and his twisted face in Cameron Crowe's *Vanilla Sky* (2001). In *M:I-2*, John Woo brings a sharp blade to within a millimetre of Cruise's eye; in Spielberg's film, the eye is actually removed. Spielberg also recreates literally the poster image of Brian De Palma's first *Mission: Impossible* (1996), Tom Cruise's smooth profile, and grafts onto it a twin face (that of the precog Agatha), turning him into a two-headed monster. A chimera.

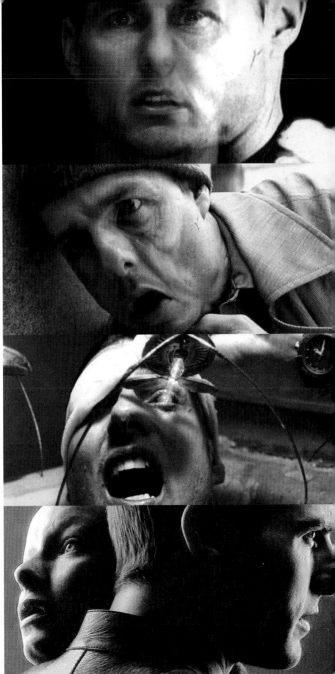

Opposite page: Samantha Morton and Tom Cruise in *Minority Report* (2002).

Above: Haley Joel Osment in *Artificial Intelligence: A.I.* (2001).

Above right: Tom Cruise and Samantha Morton in *Minority Report* (2002).

Leonardo DiCaprio in *Catch Me If You Can* (2002).

Pink candy, black heart

In the middle of this dark period there is an (apparently) lighter interlude, two 'bubbles' of comedy: *Catch Me If You Can* (2002), a champagne bubble, and *The Terminal* (2004), a glass bubble. The subject itself of *Catch Me If You Can* is highly cinematic; it is the true story of Frank Abagnale Jr, a teenage runaway and master of the art of creating false identities, who passed himself off in turn as an airline pilot, doctor and lawyer, while stealing millions of dollars. In short, like Spielberg, an expert *entertainer*. This colourful, exhilarating film is a celebration of the laid-back 1960s, full of cars with fancy bodywork, girls with bouffant skirts and back-combed hair, the heyday of PanAm and James Bond as played by Sean Connery, the pop cheekiness of

Blake Edwards's films and the chromium-plated elegance of Richard Quine's. It is a real lesson in style, taken in his stride by the dazzling Leonardo DiCaprio, a magician who plays tricks with his own face, changing his age as if changing his shirt, with nothing more than a wink. Rarely had Spielberg appeared to enjoy so much filming the actor with whom he was working.

With its ease, pace and speed, the film itself was shot like a conjuring trick, a con, filmed in 52 days and on 147 locations, from Los Angeles to New York and in Canada. Spielberg had never worked as fast, sometimes shooting on three different sets in one day. But who on earth was Spielberg talking to with his teasing 'Catch me if you can'? Himself, probably, since there are so many autobiographical

elements in the many nooks and crannies of the film. In addition to the fact that the hectic pace of filming reminded Spielberg of his apprenticeship in television, the character of Frank is an imaginary 'portrait of the artist as a young man', in the days when he would make his way into Universal Studios, with his over-large suit and empty briefcase. But the film's vibrant colours and jazzy rhythms, and Frank's vivacity, all conceal something obviously sadder — his parents' separation, the original cause of his flight. The character's accelerated ageing also springs from there, like the series of fictions he creates for himself, imaginary refuges of the same kind as Elliott's extraterrestrial friend in *E.T.* At the beginning of the film the parents are still waltzing affectionately together, watched tenderly by their son, but when the father (Christopher Walken, playing an unlucky swindler) is caught out in tax fraud, the mother (Nathalie Baye) leaves him, and her haste to get involved with another man means that she soon forgets Frank. A lost child, an inadequate father and an undeserving mother (there she is again), the Spielbergian motifs come thick and fast. Like the hero of *Minority Report*, Frank is looking for a single image: the memory of a long-ago dance in the family's living-room.

A magnificent scene expresses all this very well, when Frank comes running out of a plane just as it has landed, to turn up outside the impressive house where his mother is now living with her new husband and child — a little girl. The elegance of the flight and the burden of the loss, all the beauty of *Catch Me If You Can* is condensed in this very simple sequence of a few shots. Looking at them through the window, Frank sees the Norman Rockwell painting that Jamie dragged with him everywhere in *Empire of the Sun* come to life in flesh and blood. Compared with this model family, who are perfectly at home in their setting, he is condemned to

the spectator's seat, always outside, 'his forehead pressed against the glass like those who keep watch over sorrow.'[29]

It was no accident that Spielberg chose Tom Hanks, the oafish cop in *Catch Me If You Can*, and shut him up in an airport for the whole length of a film. The America of *Catch Me If You Can* was wide open to every audacious scheme, lying ripe for Leonardo DiCaprio's taking; in *The Terminal* it is locked down tight. 'America is closed' is the film's leitmotif; something that is constantly being said to Viktor Navorski (Tom Hanks), whose country, the fictional Krakozhia, has been erased from the map following a coup while he is on a flight to New York. As a stateless person he can neither return to his temporarily non-existent country nor enter the United States, for precisely the same reason. It is a flaw in the system that allows this to happen, in an absurdist fable set in a world reminiscent of Jacques Tati: the ubiquitous notices and direction signs, and a man exposed to the planners' world of an international transit zone. This bureaucratic nightmare is, of course, only a means by which to present the essence of America, as contained in this terminal building at JFK, New York City, the historical port of entry for immigrants to the United States.

When Viktor finally leaves the airport, with its multifarious communities and its pitfalls, he stays in New York for only a few hours; he has already seen America. He has even lived the American dream, found a job, earned money, seduced and lost a pretty woman, and he has become the hero of the terminal. Unlike Leonardo DiCaprio, who flitted from place to place following his every whim, Tom Hanks is forced to stay put, falling into the traps that this seemingly transparent world, with its glittering boutiques, puts in his path, from slippery floor surfaces to deceptive panes of glass. Spielberg makes a direct contrast between the carefree 1960s, when people did not bother to lock their doors, and the present-day sclerosis of America and its inward-looking obsession with security, in a fable that is quietly savage, and more serious than it has been given credit for.

America and the world: anxiety

In the space of five years (between 2001 and 2005), Spielberg directed no fewer than six films — film following film at almost indecently short intervals. The last two, *War of the Worlds* and *Munich*, were released six months apart and yet they in no

way suggest works cobbled together in haste. Both of them are staggering, full of turbulent action, and combine a dizzying mastery perfected over the years with a new desire to describe — which is not to say to understand — today's world. Science fiction (Martians attack the planet) is followed by history (the assassination of Israeli athletes at the 1972 Munich Olympic Games), but this is in order to look more closely at, and to film as directly as possible, a confused and uncertain present. These are two films with blood rushing through their veins.

Spielberg has explained that he made *War of the Worlds* because he believed that the story's time had come — again.[30] When he was preparing to make the film, he recalled the films about invasions from outer space that he had seen as a

child, crude or subtle parables about the threat of communism, all governed by the totemic injunction, 'Watch the skies!'[31] In 2005, the nature of the threat was much less clear: it was latent, and no longer came from the skies but from the centre of the Earth, having patiently bided its time before bursting out of the ground in an unforgettable scene, near the beginning of the film, in which the first Tripod emerges. Tom Cruise, among the crowd, is frozen with fascination at what is happening, unable to take his eyes off the horror, before he starts to run for his life. People look upwards, as if magnetized, a camera continues to film the catastrophe from the ground where it has fallen, and walls are covered with 'missing person' notices; the collective trauma of the attacks on the Twin Towers

haunts each of these shots. And then there are the images of exodus, human beings herded into 'pods' like cattle, the ashes of victims vaporized before his eyes with which Tom Cruise gradually becomes covered, and finally the burning train that bursts into the frame, a reminder of humanity's burning past in showers of sparks and snow. It is easy to hear the words 'extermination' and 'We're under attack', Shoah and 9/11; *War of the Worlds* represents a desperate attempt to combine the imagery of all the catastrophes of the twentieth and early twenty-first centuries. Spielberg has at last found the right distance; he makes a century's images pass before the eyes of one man.

In the person of Tom Cruise, an anti-hero fleeing with his two children, whom he hardly knows, Spielberg has invented the domestic disaster movie: family and chaos, the chaos of the family. In *War of the Worlds*, as in *Munich*, the approach is anything but monumental, there are no more high vantage points, no horizon. It is impossible to know what lies 'behind the hill'. Spielberg, a seasoned maker of edifying disaster movies, American-style (he produced Jan de Bont's *Twister* in 1996 and

Mimi Leder's *Deep Impact* in 1998), now chooses to abandon its codes: there are no historic monuments reduced to dust, no destruction of Manhattan, no generals studying a map of the world, no alarmist newsflashes. This is a first-person story, told as if the character was wearing blinkers, and through hearsay, and it is consequently more disturbing, in a different way. The film contains nothing that is outside Tom Cruise's field of vision. Or then it is unbearable, as when his daughter slips out of his sight for a moment (he has just told her, 'Stay there where I can see you!') and comes to a river down which heaps of dead bodies are being swept. In the first few minutes of the film, however, he had forced her to watch the strange, spell-binding storm breaking over the town; childish and unaware, he was not yet a real father. He would spend the rest of the film trying to mend this fault, obsessed with the importance of covering her eyes, in order to protect her from chaos, holding at arm's length, as if grafted to his side, this frighteningly pale little creature who is more mature than he is. (She is played by Dakota Fanning, a tremendously good actress.) His son, who is older, quickly decides to remove himself from

Eric Bana, Mathieu Kassovitz, Ciarán Hinds, Hanns Zischler and Daniel Craig in *Munich* (2005).

this protective vigilance; with his love of heroes, the exact opposite of his father, he is eager to do battle, to fight. Hardly has he disappeared behind the hill when it bursts into flames. To disappear from view is to die. And the miraculous return of the teenage son in the final scene does nothing to dissipate this sombre conviction. *War of the Worlds* is a stormy work, in which Spielberg, in the wake of his character, treads the American soil (a concept so frequently invoked and so fiercely protected) invaded by blood-red 'weeds' that make it impassable: a territory they no longer recognize.

Just like the bits of America we see in *War of the Worlds*, the Europe of *Munich* flashes past our eyes — Paris, London, Rome, Athens. Led by the taciturn Avner Kaufmann (Eric Bana), the five agents recruited by Israel to avenge the Munich murders (an eye for an eye, a tooth for a tooth), pass through cities without seeing them, blinded as much by their mission of revenge as by the instructions they

receive in dribs and drabs. The only full city-scape is the last sequence in the film: the Manhattan skyline, digitally retouched and watched over by the Twin Towers, the one symbolic element in a film that, far from the blinkered hotchpotch it was accused of being, tries to tell the story (rather than the history) of modern terrorism, blankly and, as it were, in reverse, like a photographic negative.

The DVD of *Munich*[32] opens with an introduction by Spielberg: 'We should make no mistake. I am not attacking Israel with this film.' It is an astonishing piece of self-justification when we know that in France the film was sometimes described as a piece of Israeli propaganda. Yes, but that is just the point. At exactly the same time, in the United States and in connection with the same film, Spielberg had been accused of being anti-Israel. This disparity in the way it was received demonstrates the great complexity of a film that constantly interrogates itself and its subject, building on a foundation of

Steven Spielberg on the set of *Munich* (2005).

Eric Bana and Geoffrey Rush in *Munich* (2005).

gaps rather than of facts. It is the opacity of the top-secret punitive mission orchestrated by Mossad that makes it a perfect subject for a film. 'We inhabit a world of intersecting secrecies. We live and die at the places where those secrecies meet,' is what Michael Lonsdale, a French informer with the look of an ogre, nicknamed 'Papa', tells Avner. The fiction develops in the interstices left by the tectonic plates of History, and if there is a documentary aim in *Munich*, it is only to make a documentary about uncertainty.

One by one, Avner's men die, victims of violence and reprisals, but also consumed by their feelings of helplessness, as the plot inches its way forwards, with its grainy images, tangled intelligence networks, signs and threats that cannot be interpreted, a Babel of languages and accents. The world is reduced to one great tailing operation, as the characters perpetually stake out their targets, sitting in cars over which glides the light reflected from the street. It is a curious work, not without a few moments of light relief, such as the team's meals, or a picture-postcard Paris. *Munich* is a shifting, sliding film, unwinding as its certainties start to disintegrate. There is no heroism about the executions, which are constantly thwarted — delayed by a technicality, by the unexpected appearance on the scene of a small girl, or by a badly constructed bomb that fails to explode. These clumsy, depressed 007s (the actor Daniel Craig, the current James Bond, is among the Mossad crew) are forced to make the streets their risky territory, because the houses in this sleepless film are booby-trapped; Avner, a prey to paranoia, falls asleep in a cupboard after cutting up his mattress in search of a bomb. (This parallels *War of the Worlds*, in which Tom Cruise finds the engine of a burning Boeing 747 in the living-room of a comfortable suburban home.)

The ultimate home, of course, is the nation. And it, too, is booby-trapped. The figures of Avner's mother, who sent him to a kibbutz as a small baby, and Golda Meir, who abandons him to the mission

she imposes (and tells him so), overlap. The character's private life is one of twofold detachment: detachment from ties of blood and ties to the community, and detachment from the mother and from Meir (Avner moves to New York at the end of *Munich*). 'Your mother abandoned you, now you think Israel is your mother,' Avner's wife tells him at the beginning of the film. The words are an echo of those of Tom Cruise to his son, who wanted to fight alongside the army in *War of the Worlds*: 'I know it seems like you have to fight but you don't!' Spielberg is questioning patriotism, the Founding Fathers and the mother country.

The breakdown of the maternal bond is accompanied in *Munich* by a startling innovation for Spielberg: sex scenes. The eternal teenager, the 'virgin' director, marches into the sexual breach with hot-headed clumsiness; the parallel editing of the execution of the Israeli athletes by the members of Black September and a physical love scene between Avner, his face twisted with pain, and his wife, attracted quite a bit of comment. Since the moment in 1975 when *Jaws* gave Spielberg the luxury of the director's cut, the former child prodigy has never been afraid to shoot scenes that are at the limits: the shower episode in *Schindler's List*, of course, and the poetic image of the explosion of the atom bomb in *Empire of the Sun*. Imagining scenes, trying them out, constructing shots, experimenting, going in all guns blazing, even if one scene destroys a film's perfection: the desire to grapple with cinema is astonishingly alive in this contradictory control freak. The 'reconciliatory' endings of *War of the Worlds* and *A.I.* were also disparaged, seen as reflecting Spielberg's fundamental inability to attain gravity. And yet …

The end of the happy ending

Munich, a weary film, ends on the word 'no'. But the day that David the 'mecha' was allowed to spend with his mother in *A.I.*, the return *ex machina* of Tom Cruise to confound the guilty parties in

Minority Report, or the family 'reunion' at the end of *War of the Worlds* were only foretastes of this refusal to reach a happy ending. The reveries of a child at the bottom of the sea or the delirium of a cop kept in a state of cerebral inactivity, these are unattached moments of unreal calm, but necessarily seen after death.

In the final minutes of *War of the Worlds*, the character stands at a distance from the Boston home where the whole family, his ex-wife and her parents, are watching him from the front steps. Only his son comes forward to meet him, proof that the vanished teenager is indeed a hallucination on his father's part. The grandparents are played by Gene Barry and Ann Robinson, the two leading actors in the 1953 version of H. G. Wells's novel, directed by George Pal and Byron Haskins. Unlike the pilot in *Always* who was still pouring his old skills into the ear of his young apprentice, Spielberg acknowledges, on the features of Tom Cruise, that he will never be able to match the old methods of making films. All the more reason, then, to put himself on the line with every new film.

In the final minutes of *Munich*, we are blinded by the sight of a recreated Manhattan skyline, but have we ever really looked at what is going on in the foreground? Avner and his contact, Ephraim, are talking in a derelict playground among the wrecks of roundabouts and slides. This is what has become of the digital dinosaur park, the roller-coasters of *Indiana Jones* and the imaginary land of Peter Pan. 'Maybe the child in all of us dies just when we need him the most',[33] said the man who made *E.T.*, when *Munich* was released. Since then, he seems to have embarked on a new phase of his career; with *Indiana Jones and the Kingdom of the Crystal Skull* and *The Adventures of Tintin*, he appears to have gone back to more family-orientated films. But it is my guess that the child who has died in Steven Spielberg will yet whisper some beautiful, sad, grown-up films in his ear.

96   Steven Spielberg on the set of *Close Encounters of the Third Kind* (1977).

Chronology

1946
18 December. Steven Allan Spielberg born at the Jewish Hospital, Cincinnati, Ohio. His father, Arnold, is an electronic engineer, later specializing in IT. His mother, Leah, is a concert pianist, but gives up her career to take care of her family.

1949
Birth of his sister Anne.

1952
The Spielberg family moves to Haddon Township, a suburb of Camden, New Jersey.

1953
Birth of his sister Susan.

1956
Birth of his sister Nancy.

1957
Spielberg makes his first amateur film, *The Last Train Wreck* (3 mins, 8mm). The family moves to Arcadia, Arizona.

1958 – 61
Spielberg makes a series of increasingly sophisticated amateur films, including *The Last Gunfight*, *A Day in the Life of Thunder*, *Fighter Squad*, *Film Noir* and *Scary Hollow*.

1962
Spielberg wins a competition for amateurs with *Escape to Nowhere*, a 40-minute war film.

1964
Public showing of *Firelight* (140 min) at the Phoenix Little Theater, Phoenix, Arizona. The family moves to California and settles in Saratoga.

1965 – 69
Spielberg enrols at California State University, Long Beach, where he is a somewhat casual student. He applies twice to the prestigious School of Theater, Film and Television at USC (University of Southern California), but is rejected both times. He spends time on the set of John Cassavetes's *Faces*, as an (uncredited) production assistant.

1966
His parents divorce.

1968
Makes and produces *Amblin'*, a 35mm short that wins an award at the 1969 Atlanta Film Festival.

1969
Sid Sheinberg, vice-president in charge of production at Universal Studios, offers Spielberg a seven-year contract. He leaves the university to become a professional film director.

1969 – 73
Spielberg makes a dozen or so television films or episodes.

1971
Duel is broadcast on ABC, in the series 'ABC Movie of the Weekend'. It is shown in European cinemas the following year.

1974
Release of *The Sugarland Express*, his first feature film.

1978
First Oscar nomination for best director, for *Close Encounters of the Third Kind*. (Spielberg was also nominated for *Raiders of the Lost Ark* in 1982, *E.T.* in 1983 and *The Color Purple* in 1986, but did not win his first Oscar until 1994, for *Schindler's List*.)

1982
The *E.T.* phenomenon. The film will gross $701 million worldwide, taking $11.8 million in its first weekend in the United States. Spielberg is a wealthy man. He sets up his own production company, Amblin Entertainment, with his associates Kathleen Kennedy and Frank Marshall.

1985
Birth of Spielberg's son Max and marriage to the actress Amy Irving.

1987
Wins the Irving G. Thalberg Memorial Award, a prize for producers awarded at the Oscars ceremony.

1989
Spielberg's very public divorce from Amy Irving, involving astronomical sums of money.

1990
Marries Kate Capshaw, the heroine of *Indiana Jones and the Temple of Doom*. They have their first child, a daughter, Sasha, and adopt an African–American son, Theo.

1992
Birth of Spielberg's son Sawyer.

1994
Spielberg wins the Oscar for best director, for *Schindler's List*. He launches his multimedia studio, DreamWorks SKG, with his associates Jeffrey Katzenberg and David Geffen. DreamWorks SKG is the first new Hollywood studio in 75 years. In addition to making films, the studio plans to enter the fields of animation, music, television and video games. Spielberg also sets up the Survivors of the Shoah Visual History Foundation. The TV series *ER*, produced by DreamWorks, opens on NBC. It has brought Spielberg, as he has said himself, more money than all his other successful films, colossal though they were.

1996
Birth of a daughter, Destry, and adoption of Mikaela, another African–American child. With Jessica, Kate Capshaw's daughter from a previous marriage, Spielberg now has a family of seven children. *Forbes* magazine reports that he is the second richest person in show business after Oprah Winfrey.

1998
Oscar for best director, for *Saving Private Ryan*. Jonathan Norman is sentenced to life imprisonment, of which he must serve at least twenty-five years, for harassing Spielberg.

2006
Sale of DreamWorks SKG to Viacom, which also owns Paramount Pictures. The price is said to be approximately $1.6 billion. The animation division, the most profitable, with *Antz*, *Shrek* 1 and 2, *Madagascar*, etc., remains independent, but films made by DreamWorks Animation SKG are distributed worldwide by Paramount.

2008
Four weeks before work starts on *The Adventures of Tintin: The Secret of the Unicorn*, Universal, Spielberg's long-standing partner, pulls out. At the last minute, he secures a distribution agreement from Sony Pictures, to relaunch the project.

2009
At the annual Golden Globes ceremony, Spielberg receives the Cecil B. DeMille Award, an honorary prize for Lifetime Achievement, conferred by Martin Scorsese. Following a drama lasting several months, Spielberg and his associate Stacey Snider relaunch DreamWorks, once again an independent studio (the Viacom/Paramount experiment having come to a sudden end), thanks to a financial arrangement between Reliance Big Entertainment (with Indian capital) and Disney.

Steven Spielberg with Richard Dreyfuss and François Truffaut on the set of *Close Encounters of the Third Kind* (1977).

Steven Spielberg (centre) in 1961.

Steven Spielberg in 1975.

Steven Spielberg with George Lucas in 1989.

Filmography

AMATEUR FILMS

The Last Train Wreck 1957
Format 8mm.
Running time 3 mins.
A Day in the Life 1958
of Thunder
Format 8mm.
The Last Gun 1959
Format 8mm.
Running time 8 mins.
Fighter Squad 1961
Format 8mm.
Running time 8 mins.
Scary Hollow 1961
Format 8mm.
Film of a high-school play.
Escape to Nowhere 1961
Format 8mm.
Running time 40 mins.
Firelight 1964
Format 8mm. Running time 2h 15.
With Robert Robyn, Beth Weber,
Lucky Lohr, Margaret Peyou.
Senior Sneak Day 1965
Format 8mm.
Encounter 1965–66
Format 16mm.
Running time 20 mins.
The Great Race 1966
Format 16mm.
Slipstream 1967
Format 35mm. With Jim Baxes, Tony
Bill, Roger Ernest. Unfinished.
Amblin' 1968
Format 35mm. Running time 26
mins. With Richard Levin, Pamela
McMyler.

SHORT FILMS

Kick the Can 1983
Running time 10 mins. With Scatman
Crothers, Bill Quinn, Martin Garner,
Christopher Eisenmann. Second
segment of Twilight Zone: The Movie,
directed by Steven Spielberg, John
Landis (prologue and segment 1), Joe
Dante (segment 3) and George Miller
(segment 4). In the episode made
by Spielberg, an old man (Scatman
Crothers) arrives at a retirement
home and offers the residents the
chance to relive their youth, by means
of a magic game. After the experi-
ment, they all decide to return to their
real age. Apart from one…
The Unfinished 1999
Journey
Running time 21 mins. With Maya
Angelou, Bill Clinton. Documentary.
A Timeless Call 2008
Running time 7 mins. With Tom
Hanks, Toby Meuli. A short film

for the 2008 Democratic National
Convention.

TELEVISION FILMS

'Eyes' 1969
Running time 1h 35. With Joan
Crawford. An episode of Night
Gallery.
'The Daredevil Gesture' 1970
Running time 1h. With Robert
Young. An episode of Marcus
Welby, M.D.
Duel 1971
Running time 1h 13. With Dennis
Weaver. Broadcast by ABC on 13
November 1971, in the 'ABC Movie
of the Weekend' slot. A longer ver-
sion, running for 1h 31, with addi-
tional scenes shot by Spielberg in
1972, was shown in European cin-
emas in 1972/1973.
'Eulogy for a Wide
Receiver' 1971
Running time 1h. With Arthur
Hill. An episode of Owen Marshall,
Counselor at Law.
'L.A. 2017' 1971
Running time 1h 14. With Gene
Barry. An episode of The Name of
the Game.
'Make Me Laugh' 1971
Running time 1h. With Godfrey
Cambridge. An episode of Night
Gallery.
'Murder by the Book' 1971
Running time 1h. With Peter Falk.
The first episode of Columbo.
'Par for the Course' 1971
Running time 1h. With Luther Adler.
An episode of The Psychiatrist.
'The Private World of Martin
Dalton' 1971
Running time 1h. With Pamelyn
Ferdin. An episode of The
Psychiatrist.
Something Evil 1972
Running time 1h 13. With Sandy
Dennis, Darren McGavin.
Savage 1973
Running time 73 mins. With Martin
Landau, Barbara Bain, Will Geer.
'Ghost Train' 1985
Running time 25 mins. With
Roberts Blossom. An episode of
Amazing Stories.
'The Mission' 1985
Running time 46 mins. With Kevin
Costner. An episode of Amazing
Stories. 'The Mission' also forms
part of the composite film Amazing
Stories: The Movie, released in 1987.
The other segments were made by
Robert Zemeckis and William Dear.

PRODUCER ONLY

I Wanna Hold 1978
Your Hand
by Robert Zemeckis
Used Cars 1980
by Robert Zemeckis
Continental Divide 1981
by Michael Apted
Poltergeist 1982
by Tobe Hooper
Gremlins 1984
by Joe Dante
Fandango 1985
by Kevin Reynolds
The Goonies 1985
by Richard Donner
Back to the Future 1985
by Robert Zemeckis
Young Sherlock 1985
Holmes
by Barry Levinson
The Money Pit 1986
by Richard Benjamin
An American Tail 1986
by Don Bluth
Harry and 1987
the Hendersons
by William Dear
Innerspace 1987
by Joe Dante
Three O'Clock High 1987
by Phil Joanou
*batteries 1987
not included
by Matthew Robbins
Who Framed 1988
Roger Rabbit
by Robert Zemeckis
The Land Before Time 1988
by Don Bluth
Tummy Trouble 1989
by Rob Minkoff
Dad 1989
by Gary David Goldberg
Back to the Future 1989
Part II
by Robert Zemeckis
Joe Versus 1990
the Volcano
by John Patrick Shanley
Dreams 1990
by Akira Kurosawa
Back to the Future 1990
Part III
by Robert Zemeckis
Roller Coaster Rabbit 1990
by Rob Minkoff
Gremlins 2: 1990
The New Batch
by Joe Dante
Arachnophobia 1990
by Frank Marshall
Cape Fear 1991
by Martin Scorsese

An American Tail: 1991
Fievel Goes West
by Phil Nibbelink, Simon Wells
We're Back! 1993
A Dinosaur's Story
by Phil Nibbelink, Simon Wells,
Dick Zondag, Ralph Zondag
The Flintstones 1994
by Brian Levant
Casper 1995
by Brad Silberling
Balto 1995
by Simon Wells
Twister 1996
by Jan de Bont
The Lost Children 1997
of Berlin
by Elizabeth McIntyre
Men in Black 1997
by Barry Sonnenfeld
Deep Impact 1998
by Mimi Leder
The Mask of Zorro 1998
by Martin Campbell
The Last Days 1998
by James Moll
The Haunting 1999
by Jan de Bont
Wakko's Wish 1999
by Liz Holzman, Rusty Mills
and Tom Ruegger
A Holocaust szemei 2000
by János Szász
Shrek 2001
by Andrew Adamson and
Vicky Jenson
Evolution 2001
by Ivan Reitman
Price for Peace 2002
by James Moll
Men in Black II 2002
by Barry Sonnenfeld
Voices from the List 2004
by Michael Mayhew
The Legend of Zorro 2005
by Martin Campbell
Memoirs of a Geisha 2005
by Rob Marshall
Monster House 2006
by Gil Kenan
Spell Your Name 2006
by Sergey Bukovsky
Flags of Our Fathers 2006
by Clint Eastwood
Letters from Iwo Jima 2006
by Clint Eastwood
Transformers 2007
by Michael Bay
Eagle Eye 2008
by D.J. Caruso
Transformers: 2009
Revenge of the Fallen
by Michael Bay
The Lovely Bones 2009
by Peter Jackson

FEATURE FILMS

Duel — 1971

Screenplay Richard Matheson. **Cinematography** Jack A. Marta. **Editor** Frank Morriss. **Music** Billy Goldenberg. **Producer** George Eckstein. **Production** Universal Pictures. **Running time** 1h 30. With Dennis Weaver (David Mann), Jacqueline Scott (Mrs Mann), Eddie Firestone (The bar-owner).

• On the roads of California, a car-driver is relentlessly pursued by a tanker.

The Sugarland Express — 1974

Screenplay Hal Barwood, Matthew Robbins. **Cinematography** Vilmos Zsigmond. **Editor** Edward M. Abroms, Verna Fields. **Music** John Williams. **Producers** David Brown, Richard D. Zanuck. **Production** Universal Pictures. **Running time** 1h 49. With Goldie Hawn (Lou Jean Poplin), Ben Johnson (Captain Tanner), William Atherton (Clovis Poplin), Michael Sacks (Slide).

• Lou Jean persuades her husband to abscond from prison, although he is due to be released shortly, and go in search of their baby, who has been placed with a foster family in Sugarland, Texas. They kidnap a police officer with his car, and are pursued by the forces of law and order.

Jaws — 1975

Screenplay Peter Benchley, Carl Gottlieb. **Cinematography** Bill Butler. **Editor** Verna Fields. **Music** John Williams. **Producers** David Brown, Richard D. Zanuck. **Production** Universal Pictures. **Running time** 2h 04. With Roy Scheider (Martin Brody), Richard Dreyfuss (Matt Hooper), Robert Shaw (Quint), Lorraine Gary (Ellen Brody), Murray Hamilton (Larry Vaughn).

• The police chief Martin Brody clashes with the town's mayor, who refuses to close its beaches, although there is no doubt that a shark is attacking holidaymakers and spreading terror through the peaceful seaside resort of Amity.

Close Encounters of the Third Kind — 1977

Screenplay Steven Spielberg. **Cinematography** Vilmos Zsigmond. **Editor** Michael Kahn. **Music** John Williams. **Producers** Julia Phillips, Michael Phillips, Clark L. Paylow. **Production** Columbia Pictures Corporation. **Running time** 2h 15. With Richard Dreyfuss (Roy Neary), Teri Garr (Ronnie Neary), Melinda Dillon (Julian Guiler), François Truffaut (Claude Lacombe).

• A series of strange events take place around the world, and especially in Indiana, where a UFO appears to Roy Neary, and to other residents. Obsessed by this experience and haunted by the image of a mountain, Neary goes to Devils Tower, Wyoming, where, with a number of others (a military and scientific team led by the Frenchman Claude Lacombe), he finally has an encounter of the third kind.

1941 — 1979

Screenplay Bob Gale, Bob Zemeckis, based on an idea by Gale, Zemeckis and John Milius. **Cinematography** William Fraker. **Editor** Michael Kahn. **Music** John Williams. **Producer** Buzz Feitshans. **Executive producer** John Milius. **Production** Columbia Pictures Corporation. **Running time** 2h. With Dan Aykroyd (Sergeant Tree), Ned Beatty (Ward Douglas), John Belushi (Wild Bill Kelso), Lorraine Gary (Joan Douglas), Murray Hamilton (Claude), Christopher Lee (Von Kleinschmidt), Warren Oates (Maddox), Robert Stack (General Stilwell), Toshirô Mifune (Mitamura).

• In 1941, a Japanese submarine surfaces off Los Angeles, with the aim of capturing a stronghold called Hollywood. In the city itself, resistance, or more correctly, panic, is organized.

Raiders of the Lost Ark — 1981

Screenplay Lawrence Kasdan, from a story by George Lucas and Philip Kaufman. **Cinematography** Douglas Slocombe. **Editor** Michael Kahn. **Music** John Williams. **Producers** Frank Marshall, George Lucas, Howard G. Kazanjian. **Production** Lucasfilm Ltd., Paramount Pictures. **Running time** 1h 53. With Harrison Ford (Indiana Jones), Karen Allen (Marion Ravenwood), Paul Freeman (René Belloq), John Rhys-Davies (Sallah).

• In 1936, Indiana Jones, an archaeology professor in his working life and treasure-hunter in the jungle, is hired by the U.S. secret service to attempt to recover, before the Nazis do so, the Ark of the Covenant, a relic with magical powers said to have contained the Tablets of the Law given to Moses on Mount Sinai, which Hitler wants to get his hands on.

E.T.: The Extra-Terrestrial — 1982

Screenplay Melissa Mathison. **Cinematography** Allen Daviau. **Editor** Carol Littleton. **Music** John Williams. **Producers** Kathleen Kennedy, Melissa Mathison, Steven Spielberg. **Production** Universal Pictures, Amblin Entertainment. **Running time** 2h 01. With Henry Thomas (Elliott), Dee Wallace (Mary), Peter Coyote (Keys), Robert MacNaughton (Michael), Drew Barrymore (Gertie).

• A little extraterrestrial, whose flying saucer took off suddenly, leaving him alone in the outskirts of Los Angeles, takes refuge in the garage of a suburban home. The younger boy of the household, ten-year-old Elliott, finds and befriends him, and decides at first to keep his presence secret.

Indiana Jones and The Temple of Doom — 1984

Screenplay Willard Huyck, Gloria Katz. **Cinematography** Douglas Slocombe. **Editor** Michael Kahn. **Music** John Williams. **Producers** Robert Watts, George Lucas, Kathleen Kennedy, Frank Marshall. **Production** Lucasfilm Ltd., Paramount Pictures. **Running time** 1h 58. With Harrison Ford (Indiana Jones), Kate Capshaw (Willie Scott), Jonathan Ke Huy Quan (Demi-lune), Amrish Puri (Mola Ram).

• 1935: in India, a mysterious sect has abducted all the children of a village, as well as the magic stone that guaranteed them water and prosperity. Indiana Jones agrees to find them, accompanied by a nightclub singer and a little boy.

The Color Purple — 1985

Screenplay Alice Walker, Menno Meyjes, from the novel by Alice Walker. **Cinematography** Allen Daviau. **Editor** Michael Kahn. **Music** Quincy Jones. **Producers** Kathleen Kennedy, Frank Marshall, Quincy Jones. **Production** Warner Bros., Amblin Entertainment, Gubers-Peters Company. **Running time** 2h 32. With Whoopi Goldberg (Celie), Danny Glover (Mr Albert), Margaret Avery (Shug Avery), Oprah Winfrey (Sofia).

• 1909–1937: thirty years in the life of Celie, a young Black girl abused by her stepfather, deprived of her two children, separated from her sister and forced to marry a violent, tyrannical husband.

Empire of the Sun — 1987

Screenplay J.G. Ballard, Tom Stoppard, from the novel by J.G. Ballard. **Cinematography** Allen Daviau. **Editor** Michael Kahn. **Music** John Williams. **Producers** Kathleen Kennedy, Frank Marshall, Steven Spielberg. **Production** Warner Bros., Amblin Entertainment. **Running time** 2h 34. With Christian Bale (Jamie), John Malkovich (Basie), Miranda Richardson (Mrs Victor), Nigel Havers (Dr Rawlins), Joe Pantoliano (Frank Demarest).

• It is 1941, and Japan is occupying China. James Graham, a ten-year-old boy, son of a British businessman, is leading a peaceful life in the international concession in Shanghai. But the conflict intensifies and James is separated from his parents when the city is captured by the Japanese army. Through a series of misadventures, he ends up in a prisoner-of-war camp, where he has to learn to survive alone for several years.

Indiana Jones and the Last Crusade 1989

Screenplay Jeffrey Boam. **Cinematography** Douglas Slocombe. **Editor** Michael Kahn. **Music** John Williams. **Producers** Robert Watts, Frank Marshall, George Lucas. **Production** Lucasfilm Ltd., Paramount Pictures. **Running time** 2h 05. With Harrison Ford (Indiana Jones), Sean Connery (Professeur Henry Jones Sr), Denholm Elliott (Marcus Borody), Alison Doody (Elsa Schneider), John Rhys-Davies (Sallah), River Phoenix (Indiana as a young boy).
• This time, the archaeologist goes in search of the Holy Grail. One innovation: his father, with whom he lost contact many years ago, accompanies him on this new adventure. And supposing the Grail was in fact a father's love?

Always 1989

Screenplay Jerry Belson from original film. **Cinematography** Mikael Salomon. **Editor** Michael Kahn. **Music** John Williams. **Producers** Kathleen Kennedy, Frank Marshall, Steven Spielberg. **Production** Universal Pictures, Amblin Entertainment. **Running time** 2h 04. With Richard Dreyfuss (Pete Sandich), Holly Hunter (Dorinda Durston), Brad Johnson (Ted Baker), John Goodman (Al Yackey), Audrey Hepburn (Hap).
• Pete is an air-ace, a flying firefighter and an incorrigible daredevil. Each of his missions is a nightmare for Dorinda, his girlfriend. It was bound to happen: one day, he doesn't come back. Or rather, he comes back, but nobody sees him. His ghost then guides through their mourning those who are left behind. The

film is a remake of Victor Fleming's *A Guy Named Joe* (1943; screenplay by Dalton Trumbo).

Hook 1991

Screenplay James V. Hart, Malia Scotch Marmo, from a story by Hart and Nick Castle, based on J. M. Barrie's play *Peter Pan* and his novels *The Little White Bird*, *Peter Pan in Kensington Gardens* and *Peter and Wendy*. **Cinematography** Dean Cundey. **Editor** Michael Kahn. **Music** John Williams. **Producers** Kathleen Kennedy, Frank Marshall, Gerald R. Molen. **Production** Tristar Pictures, Columbia Pictures Corporation, Amblin Entertainment. **Running time** 2h 20. With Dustin Hoffman (Captain James Hook), Robin Williams (Peter Banning), Julia Roberts (Tinkerbell), Bob Hoskins (Smee), Maggie Smith (Wendy).
• Peter Pan has grown up. He has become a successful, down-to-earth businessman. When his children are kidnapped by Captain Hook, he is forced to recapture his childhood, and his imagination.

Jurassic Park 1993

Screenplay Michael Crichton, David Koepp, from the novel by Michael Crichton. **Cinematography** Dean Cundey. **Editor** Michael Kahn. **Music** John Williams. **Producers** Kathleen Kennedy, Gerald R. Molen. **Production** Universal Pictures, Amblin Entertainment. **Running time** 2h 07. With Sam Neill (Dr Alan Grant), Laura Dern (Dr Ellie Sattler), Jeff Goldblum (Dr Ian Malcolm), Richard Attenborough (John Parker Hammond), Bob Peck (Park warden).
• A megalomaniac multi-millionaire has successfully recreated dinosaurs, using blood preserved in a fossilized mosquito. He is about to open the world's most stunning theme park, but first invites a team of scientists to view it. Their visit turns into a nightmare.

Schindler's List 1993

Screenplay Steven Zaillian. **Cinematography** Janusz Kaminski. **Editor** Michael Kahn. **Music** John Williams. **Producers** Branko Lustig, Gerald R. Molen, Kathleen Kennedy, Steven Spielberg. **Production** Universal Pictures, Amblin Entertainment. **Running time** 3h 15. With Liam Neeson (Oskar Schindler), Ben Kingsley (Itzhak Stern), Ralph Fiennes (Amon Goeth), Jonathan Sagalle (Poldek), Embetz Davidtz (Helen Hirsch), Caroline Goodall (Emilie Schindler).
• Oskar Schindler, a complacent businessman and member of the Nazi party, employs Jews in his factory near Kraków, taking advantage of this source of cheap labour. When, in 1943, he witnesses the destruction by the Nazis of the Kraków ghetto, something in him irrevocably changes; he decides, with the help of his accountant, Itzhak Stern, to devote all his energies (and his money) to trying to keep as many Jews as he can out of the extermination camps, by negotiating with SS officers to hire them to work in his factory, and in that way to save them from being massacred.

The Lost World 1997

Screenplay Michael Crichton, David Koepp, from the novel by Michael Crichton. **Cinematography** Janusz Kaminski. **Editor** Michael Kahn. **Music** John Williams. **Producers** Gerald R. Molen, Colin Wilson. **Production** Universal Pictures, Amblin Entertainment. **Running time** 2h 09. With Jeff Goldblum (Dr Ian Malcolm), Julianne Moore (Dr Sarah Harding), Richard Attenborough (John Hammond), Arliss Howard (Peter Ludlow), Vince Vaughn (Nick Van Owen).
• Some other dinosaurs, descendants of those cloned by multi-millionaire John Hammond a few years previously, are living at large on an island near the original one. A scientific expedition is sent to study the situation, but they discover they are not the first people to arrive there.

Amistad 1997

Screenplay David H. Franzoni. **Cinematography** Janusz Kaminski. **Editor** Michael Kahn. **Music** John Williams. **Producers** Debbie Allen, Steven Spielberg, Colin Wilson. **Production** DreamWorks SKG, Home Box Office (HBO). **Running time** 2h 35. With Morgan Freeman (Theodore Joadson), Nigel Hawthorne (Martin), Anthony Hopkins (John Quincy), Djimon Hounsou (Cinque), Matthew McConaughey (Roger S. Baldwin).
• 1839: there has been a mutiny on the Amistad, a Spanish ship carrying African slaves. The slaves manage to free themselves, but the captain takes them not to Africa but to America, where they are thrown in jail. Two fervent abolitionists and a lawyer take on their defence, in a trial of great symbolic importance.

Saving Private Ryan 1998

Screenplay Robert Rodat. **Cinematography** Janusz Kaminski. **Editor** Michael Kahn. **Music** John Williams. **Producers** Ian Bryce, Mark Gordon, Gary Levinsohn, Steven Spielberg. **Production** DreamWorks SKG, Amblin Entertainment, Paramount Pictures. **Running time** 2h 50. With Tom Hanks (John H. Miller), Tom Sizemore (Michael Horvath), Edward Burs (Richard Reiben), Matt Damon (James Francis Ryan), Jeremy Davies (Timothy Upham), Vin Diesel (Adrian Caparzo).
• In 1944, the allied forces land at Omaha Beach. A squad of eight men, led by Captain Miller, is ordered to go behind enemy lines, in search of Private Ryan, who is somewhere in the Normandy countryside. His three brothers have been killed in action in different battles, and the government wants to return her last remaining son to his mother.

Artificial Intelligence: A.I. 2001

Screenplay Steven Spielberg, Ian Watson, from the short story by

Brian Aldiss, 'Supertoys Last All Summer Long'. **Cinematography** Janusz Kaminski. **Editor** Michael Kahn. **Music** John Williams. **Producers** Bonnie Curtis, Kathleen Kennedy, Steven Spielberg. **Production** Warner Bros., DreamWorks SKG, Amblin Entertainment, Stanley Kubrick Pictures. **Running time** 2h 26. With Haley Joel Osment (David Swinton), Frances O'Connor (Monica Swinton), Sam Robards (Henry Swinton), Jude Law (Gigolo Joe), William Hurt (Hobby).

• In the twenty-first century, increasingly sophisticated robots now perform domestic tasks. David, an advanced little robot capable of feelings and emotions, is sent to the home of the Swintons, whose biological child, suffering from a serious illness, is in suspended animation for the time being. When he recovers, David is abandoned.

Minority Report **2002**
Screenplay Scott Frank, Jon Cohen, from a short story by Philip K. Dick. **Cinematography** Janusz Kaminski. **Editor** Michael Kahn. **Music** John Williams. **Producers** Jan de Bont, Bonnie Curtis, Gerald R. Molen, Walter F. Parkes. **Production** 20th Century Fox, DreamWorks SKG, Cruise/Wagner, Blue Tulip Productions. **Running time** 2h 25. With Tom Cruise (John Anderton), Max Von Sydow (Lamar Burgess), Steve Harris (Jad), Colin Farrell (Danny Witwer).

• In 2054, an experimental FBI unit, called 'Precrime', has succeeded in eradicating murder by arresting the guilty parties 'before' their crime, using the visions of three teenagers with clairvoyant powers. One fine day, John Anderton, who heads the unit, sees on the screen the features of the next guilty man: himself.

Catch Me If You Can **2002**
Screenplay Jeff Nathanson, from the book by Frank Abagnale Jr and Stan Redding. **Cinematography** Janusz Kaminski. **Editor** Michael Kahn. **Music** John Williams. **Producers** Walter F. Parkes, Steven Spielberg. **Production** Dream-

Works SKG, Amblin Entertainment, Kemp Company, Parkes/MacDonald Productions. **Running time** 2h 21. With Leonardo DiCaprio (Frank Abagnale Jr), Tom Hanks (FBI agent Carl Hanratty), Christopher Walken (Frank Abagnale Sr), Nathalie Baye (Paula Abagnale).

• In the 1960s, Frank Abagnale Jr, a virtuoso teenage creator of false identities, passes himself off in turn as an airline pilot, a doctor and a lawyer, while issuing false cheques that enable him to steal millions of dollars.

The Terminal **2004**
Screenplay Sacha Gervasi and Jeff Nathanson, from a story by Andrew Niccol and Sacha Gervasi. **Cinematography** Janusz Kaminski. **Editor** Michael Kahn. **Music** John Williams. **Production** Dream Works SKG, Amblin Entertainment, Parkes/MacDonald Productions. **Running time** 2h 08. With Tom Hanks (Viktor Navorski), Catherine Zeta-Jones (Amelia Warren), Stanley Tucci (Frank Dixon), Diego Luna (Enrique Cruz).

• Viktor Navorski, a tourist, lands at JFK airport, New York. But while he was flying to the United States, there was a coup in his country, Krakozhia, temporarily erasing it from the map and making Viktor stateless. As a result, he can neither enter American soil nor go home. For an indeterminate time the airport becomes his home, his country and his prison.

War of the Worlds **2005**
Screenplay Josh Friedman, David Koepp, from the novel by H. G. Wells. **Cinematography** Janusz Kaminski. **Editor** Michael Kahn. **Music** John Williams. **Producers** Kathleen Kennedy, Colin Wilson. **Production** Paramount Pictures, DreamWorks SKG, Amblin Entertainment, Cruise/Wagner Productions. **Running time** 1h 56. With Tom Cruise (Ray Ferrier), Dakota Fanning (Rachel Ferrier), Justin Chatwin (Robbie Ferrier), Tim Robbins (Harlan Ogilvy).

• Extraterrestrials attack Earth; the Tripods tear up the soil of American cities. The day when Ray Ferrier, a divorced docker and unreliable father,

is about to play host to his two children, whom he has not seen for years, on a weekend visit, is the very one on which the apocalypse starts.

Munich **2005**
Screenplay Tony Kushner, Eric Roth, after *Vengeance* by George Jonas. **Cinematography** Janusz Kaminski. **Editor** Michael Kahn. **Music** John Williams. **Producers** Kathleen Kennedy, Colin Wilson, Barry Mendel, Steven Spielberg. **Production** Universal Pictures, DreamWorks SKG, Amblin Entertainment, Kennedy/Marshall Company. **Running time** 2h 44. With Eric Bana (Avner), Daniel Craig (Steve), Ciarán Hinds (Carl), Mathieu Kassovitz (Robert), Geoffrey Rush (Ephraim).

• On 5 September 1972, a commando of the Palestinian organization Black September kills twelve Israeli athletes during the Munich Olympic Games. Golda Meir's government mounts a top-secret reprisal operation: the young Mossad agent Avner Kaufmann and four other men are recruited to track down and eliminate eleven of the Palestinians behind the Munich massacre.

Indiana Jones and **2008**
the Kingdom of
the Crystal Skull
Screenplay David Koepp. **Cinematography** Janusz Kaminski. **Sound** Ben Burtt. **Editor** Michael Kahn. **Music** John Williams. **Producers** George Lucas, Kathy Kennedy. **Production** Paramount Pictures, LucasFilms Ltd. **Running time** 2h 03. With Harrison Ford (Indiana Jones), Cate Blanchett (Irina Spalko), Karen Allen (Marion Ravenwood), Shia LaBeouf (Mutt Williams).

• We're well into the 1950s, and the Cold War is raging before the eyes of Indiana Jones, now twenty years older. In this adventure, which pits him against a formidable Soviet scientist on the track of a mysterious skull of extraterrestrial appearance, the archaeologist with the whip finds his first love again, and discovers he has a son.

Selected Bibliography

Biskind, Peter
Easy Riders, Raging Bulls
New York,
Simon & Schuster, 1999.

Buckland, Warren
Directed by Steven Spielberg: Poetics of the Contemporary Hollywood Blockbuster
New York / London,
Continuum, 2006.

Crawley, Tony
The Steven Spielberg Story
London,
Zomba Books, 1983.

Friedman, Lester and Notbohm, Brent
Steven Spielberg Interviews
Jackson, University Press of Mississippi, 2000.

McBride, Joseph
Steven Spielberg: A Biography
New York,
Simon & Schuster, 1997.

Schickel, Richard
'Spielberg Takes on Terror'
Time Magazine,
4 December 2005.

Schickel, Richard
'His Prayer for Peace'
Time Magazine,
14 December 2005.

Notes

1. Interview with Richard Schickel, 'His Prayer for Peace', *Time* Magazine, 14 December 2005.

2. Joseph McBride, *Steven Spielberg: A Biography*, New York, Simon & Schuster, 1997.

3. Spielberg has often said that *The Bridge on the River Kwai* (1957) and *Lawrence of Arabia* (1962) are among the films that have had the most profound effect on him. David Lean himself expressed a deep admiration for the young director's talent when he saw *Duel*. When he was making *Indiana Jones and the Temple of Doom*, Spielberg shot, with a certain pride, some scenes that are not that different from the exteriors in *Lawrence of Arabia*. Indeed, *Empire of the Sun*, which Spielberg made in 1987, was originally David Lean's project.

4. Two TV films featuring police lieutenant Columbo had already been broadcast, one in 1967, the other in March 1971. The studio then decided to turn them into a regular series. Seven episodes were shot in the summer of 1971, and it was the one made by Spielberg (entitled 'Murder by the Book') that was chosen to launch the series, in September.

5. 'Filming for Spielberg', the introduction written by Truffaut for Tony Crawley's *The Steven Spielberg Story*, London, Zomba Books, 1983.

6. This 'cry', borrowed from Jack Arnold's *Creature from the Black Lagoon* (1954), was used again by Spielberg at the moment when the shark dies in *Jaws*.

7. The title of Jiminy Cricket's song in *Pinocchio*. At the end of *Close Encounters of the Third Kind*, Spielberg had the composer, John Williams, add a musical phrase from that song at the moment when the spaceship carries Richard Dreyfuss away. Earlier in the film, Dreyfuss insists that his children watch the Walt Disney cartoon. The *Pinocchio* story is only lightly touched upon here, but it is at the heart of *Artificial Intelligence: A.I.* (2001), made almost twenty-five years later.

8. Spielberg has always said that the germ of *Close Encounters of the Third Kind* lay in his childhood, when his father woke him in the middle of the night to watch a meteor shower. The scene is presented in the film in exactly the same way.

9. Bill Krohn, 'L'été de *E.T.*', *Cahiers du cinéma*, no. 342, December 1982. The internal quotation is from William Wordsworth.

10. Spielberg has known John Milius, who wrote the screenplay for Coppola's *Apocalypse Now* (1979) and directed *Conan the Barbarian* (1982), for many years, since he first began to hang out with the group of 'young Turks' who had graduated from the USC (University of Southern California) film school. Milius, with whose provocative right-wing ideas Spielberg tended to clash, made an uncredited contribution to the screenplay of *Jaws*, writing the long speech in which Quint (Robert Shaw) describes the 1945 sinking of USS *Indianapolis* in shark-infested waters. Spielberg met Robert Zemeckis in 1973, when Zemeckis asked him to look at one of his student films. He wrote the caustic script of *1941* with his buddy Robert Gale (they were known as 'the two Bobs'). With Joe Dante and a few others, Zemeckis was one of the 'protégés' whom Spielberg took under his wing, and whose films he went on to produce (the two *Gremlin* titles for Dante and the three *Back to the Future* films for Zemeckis.)

11. With his associates Jeffrey Katzenberg, former CEO at the Walt Disney Company, and David Geffen, founder of the record label Geffen Company, Spielberg's ambition was to set up a modern 'major', with a multimedia base, to develop, produce and distribute not only films but also video games, TV programmes and music. When DreamWorks SKG was founded in 1994, it was the first new Hollywood studio of any size since 20th Century Fox was set up in 1935!

12. Spielberg met George Lucas in the late 1960s, at a showing of student films, where he was greatly impressed by Lucas's science-fiction short, *THX 1138: 4EB*, and was even jealous, as he has confessed himself. They became close and, as their careers developed along parallel lines, friendly competitors. (When *Star Wars* was released in 1977, it overtook *Jaws* as the 'greatest success of all time'.) In 1979, Spielberg had just had his first failure with *1941*, and Lucas suggested Indiana Jones to him. With the help of the screenwriter Lawrence Kasdan, the two of them worked out together the dramatis personae and the assignment of roles: Spielberg would direct and Lucas produce. He was closely involved, often to be seen poring over the stills, and he also shot some second-unit sequences.

13. Indiana Jones's Bond-like ascendancy was exploited literally with the appearance in the third episode of Sean Connery as the hero's father. The origins of the trilogy thus meld with the fiction: the 'father' of the Indiana Jones series is indeed Indiana Jones's father.

14. Following the release of *Raiders of the Lost Ark*, a number of critics compared the adventures of Spielberg's archaeologist, with their clear, traditional lines, to those of Hergé's boy-reporter, enabling Spielberg, who did not know them, to discover the ever-popular Tintin books. He was immediately charmed by the Belgian cartoonist's work, and with his encouragement he planned to adapt them for the screen. The project was deferred several times and it was not until 2009, almost thirty years after he had made the acquaintance of the hero with the little quiff, that Spielberg decided that the technology was sufficiently advanced, with the development of 'performance capture', to make a *Tintin* trilogy feasible.

15. The PG-13 (Parental Guidance under 13) certificate was practically created for this film by the MPAA (Motion Picture Association of America), the body responsible for classifying films. Spielberg later admitted that he regretted what he saw as the excessively dark character of this second episode: 'I wasn't at all happy with the *Temple of Doom*,' he said in 1989. 'I thought the film was too dark, too "subterranean", much too horrific. It contains nothing that could really be called personal.'

16. Spielberg is an incorrigible fetishist, and bought at an auction the famous 'Rosebud' sledge that Welles used in the film, the name being a private code-word for lost childhood and its regrets.

17. At the time, Spielberg himself was a keen collector of work by Rockwell, the painter of American prosperity and a forerunner of hyperrealism.

18. Serge Grünberg, 'Règlements de comptes à Jurassic Park', *Cahiers du cinéma*, no. 473, November 1993.

19. The staging of the kitchen sequence in *Jurassic Park*, in which two children, pursued by the velociraptors, are saved by their own reflections in the chrome door of a cupboard, is repeated almost exactly in *War of the Worlds*, when Tom Cruise's character, hiding in a cellar with his daughter, uses a mirror to outwit the creatures hunting for them.

20. As if they had made a pact, the two men were not to leave one another. Since then, Kaminski has worked on all Spielberg's films, becoming one of his loyal collaborators, who include the editor Michael Kahn (for all the films, except *E.T.*, since *Close Encounters of the Third Kind*) and the composer John Williams (all the films since *The Sugarland Express*, except *The Color Purple*).

21. Hannah Arendt, *The Human Condition*, 1958.

22. The project was controversial from the moment it was announced; the idea that Spielberg, the so-called king of entertainment, was going to make 'a film about the Holocaust' (which is how it was described before it was even made) was unacceptable in principle, and there were fears of a 'Holocaust theme park'. When the film was released, Claude Lanzmann, the director of *Shoah* (1985), launched a violent attack against Spielberg. Lanzmann had made his over-nine-hours-long documentary without using a single archive image, and to him, any film that had passed through the 'filter' of Hollywood must necessarily trivialize the horror, destroying its unique and unimaginable character. This posed in all its clarity the problem of how the Holocaust was to be represented, the great moral and aesthetic question of the late twentieth century: can one represent – in film or literature – that is to say, in art, what one cannot oneself imagine?

23. Pierre Reverdy, 'Bonne chance ['Good Luck']', in *Sable mouvant et*

Sources

autres poèmes, Paris, Gallimard, 1951, reprinted in Poésie/Gallimard series, 2003.

24. 'Laughter is something mechanical applied to something living.'

25. Leah Spielberg interviewed by Joseph McBride, *op. cit.*

26. In Fritz Lang's film, a man who has just been found innocent inadvertently utters the victim's real name, Emma, when he is supposed to have had no way of knowing it. In *Minority Report*, the guilty man betrays himself in a similar way by saying the victim has been drowned, a detail he could not possibly have known if he was as ignorant of the affair as he claims to be.

27. See the enlightening text on this subject by Jean-Sébastien Chauvin, 'Attrape une image (si tu peux)', *Cahiers du cinéma*, no. 577, March 2003.

28. Interview in the bonus material supplied with the DVD of *Minority Report*, published by Fox Pathé Europa.

29. Paul Éluard, *L'Amour la poésie*, in Poésie/Gallimard series, Paris, Gallimard, 1929.

30. Interview in the bonus material supplied with the DVD of *War of the Worlds*, published by Paramount.

31. 'Watch the skies!', the last line of *The Thing from Another World* (1951), by Howard Hawks and Christian Nyby.

32. In the Universal edition.

33. Interviewed by Richard Schickel, *Time* Magazine, 14 December 2005.

Collection Cahiers du cinéma: cover, inside front cover, pp.2–3, 4–5, 6, 8, 26, 28, 29, 30–1, 37, 38–9, 40, 42–3, 44, 45, 46, 47, 48–9, 50–1, 53 (top), 54 (bottom), 56–7, 58–9, 60–1, 62–3, 64–5, 66–7, 68, 70, 73, 74–5, 76–7, 78 (left), 82, 83 (bottom), 86–7, 88–9, 90, 90–1, 92, 93 (bottom), 97 (2nd and 4th col.), 99 (2nd col. top; 3rd col.; 4th col. top), 100 (1st and 2nd col.; 3rd col. bottom; 4th col. top and centre), 101 (2nd col.; 3rd col. bottom).
Collection CAT'S: pp.11, 14–5, 16, 17, 18, 19, 20–1, 22, 23, 25, 27, 32–3, 34, 36, 38 (top), 43 (bottom), 52 (bottom), 53 (bottom), 54 (top), 56–7, 64, 71, 79 (right), 80, 84–5, 93 (top), 95, 99 (1st col. centre and bottom; 2nd col. bottom; 4th col. bottom), 100 (3rd col. top), 101 (1st col. bottom), inside back cover.
Martin Scorsese Collection: p.35.
Screen grabs: pp.12, 13, 52 (centre), 72, 78–9, 81, 83 (top), 99 (1st col. top).

Credits

© 20th Century Fox/DreamWorks: pp.45 (right), 74–5, 76–7, 78 (left), 80, 81 (2nd col.), 101 (1st col. top).
© Andy Warhol Estate: p.55 (right).
© Columbia Pictures/EMI Films: pp.25, 26, 27, 28, 29, inside back cover.
© Columbia/Sony Pictures: pp.8, 45 (left), 97 (2nd col.), 99 (2nd col.), 100 (2nd col. top).
© Columbia/Sony Pictures/Murray Close: pp.50–1.
© Richard Y. Hoffman Jr.: pp.9, 97 (1st col.).
© MK2/Films du Carrosse: p.53 (top).
© Norman Rockwell Estate: p.52 (top).

© Paramount/DreamWorks/Amblin: inside front cover, pp.40, 44 (left), 66–7, 68, 79 (right), 82, 83 (bottom), 84–5, 86, 86–7, 88–9, 90, 90–1, 92, 93, 95, 100 (4th col.), 101 (2nd col.; 3rd col. top).
© Paramount/Lucasfilm: pp.2–3, 42–3, 43 (bottom), 44 (right), 73, 99 (2nd col. top and bottom), 100 (1st col. top), 101 (3rd col. top).
© Photofest/Universal TV: p.10.
© Carol Royce: p.35.
© Henry Thomas: pp.38–9.
© Traverso: p.97 (3rd col.).
© United Artists/Universal/Amblin Entertainment: pp.4–5, 46, 54, 56–7, 58–9, 60–1, 62–3, 64, 64–5, 100 (1st col. centre and bottom; 2nd col. bottom; 3rd col.).
© Universal: cover, pp.6, 11, 12, 13, 14–5, 30–1, 32–3, 34, 36, 37, 38 (top), 72 (1st col.), 99 (1st col. top; 3rd col. centre).
© Universal/Zanuck/Brown Prod.: pp.16, 17, 18, 19, 20–1, 22, 23, 99 (1st col. centre and bottom).
© Warner: p.39 (right).
© Warner/DreamWorks/Amblin: pp.47, 48–9, 52 (centre and bottom), 53 (bottom), 70, 71, 72 (2nd col.), 81 (1st col.), 99 (4th col.).

All reasonable efforts have been made to trace the copyright holders of the photographs used in this book. We apologize to anyone that we were unable to reach.

Cover: *E.T.* (1982).
Inside front cover: *War of the Worlds* (2005).
Inside back cover: Cary Guffey in *Close Encounters of the Third Kind* (1977).

Acknowledgements

Fabien Suarez, Olivier Joyard, Patrice Blouin, Jean-Sébastien Chauvin, Claudine Paquot, Bill Krohn, Jonathan Wingfield.

Cahiers du cinéma Sarl
65, rue Montmartre
75002 Paris

www.cahiersducinema.com

Revised English Edition © 2010 Cahiers du cinéma Sarl
First published in French as *Steven Spielberg* © 2007 Cahiers du cinéma Sarl

ISBN 978 2 8664 2575 3

Series conceived by Claudine Paquot
Designed by Werner Jeker/Les Ateliers du Nord
Translated by Imogen Forster
Printed in China

New College Nottingham
Learning Centres